THE SALT LAKE TEMPLE

A Monument to a People

CONTENTS

I
BRIGHAM YOUNG
1801-1877
Pages 6-45

II
THE SALT LAKE TEMPLE
1853-1893
Pages 46-83

III
THE INTERIOR
Pages 84-137

IV
THE SYMBOLISM OF THE EXTERIOR
Pages 138-177

V
TEMPLE SQUARE
Pages 178-201

VI
THE ARCHITECTURAL LEGACY
Pages 202-208

FOURTH EDITION

Published in the United States of America in 1983 by
University Services Corporation
Salt Lake City, Utah
Copyright © 1983 by University Services Corporation.
Printed and bound in the United States of America.

All rights reserved.
No part of this book may be used
in any form or reproduced in any manner
—graphic, electronic or mechanical,
including photocopying, recording, taping, scanning
or information storage and retrieval systems—
by any person without written
permission of the publisher,
University Services Corporation.

ISBN 0-913535-06-0
FOURTH EDITION HARDBOUND

Library of Congress Catalog Card Number 83-81785

ACKNOWLEDGMENT

The Salt Lake Temple: A Monument to a People is based on the research and study of C. Mark Hamilton, Ph.D., Architectural History, and has been written in collaboration with the concept and design of C. Nina Cutrubus.

Dr. Hamilton's work on the Salt Lake Temple represents nine years of ongoing research that have taken him twice to England and numerous times across the United States.

Special consideration and acknowledgment is extended to the following: The Church of Jesus Christ of Latter-day Saints Copyrights and Permissions Office; the Church Historical Department for accommodating the extensive historical information; Church Graphics; Archival Libraries for permission to reproduce from all historic photograhs, the original architectural plans, and the photographic glass plates taken by C. R. Savage in 1911 depicting the interior of the Salt Lake Temple; Kaye W. Hamilton, Dr. Terrell M. Butler, Paul L. Anderson, Dr. Leonard J. Arrington, Loren D. Martin, J.D., for their perusal of the text; and to Donald T. Schmidt, William W. Slaughter, Eldon K. Linschoten, and Lorin D. Wiggins for their assistance.

I

BRIGHAM YOUNG
1801-1877

A portrait study of Brigham Young as he appeared in his later years.

BRIGHAM YOUNG
1801-1877

The Salt Lake Temple is a monument to Brigham Young, his people, and the Faith that sustained them as they were driven by persecution from New York, Ohio, Missouri, and Illinois to the desert valleys of the mountain west. Even with new temples and meetinghouses being built in ever-increasing numbers, the Salt Lake Temple remains the most important building of The Church of Jesus Christ of Latter-day Saints. When Brigham Young called for its construction within days of the Saints' arrival in the Great Basin region, he saw it as a means to rally the strength of his people during times of hardship. He envisioned it as a tangible symbol to remind the faithful of the Church of their sacred obligations before God. As its walls rose from the foundations, it gave courage and determination to over 70,000 Saints who immigrated to Utah Territory during Brigham Young's thirty-three-year tenure as the leader of the Church. After his death in 1877 it continued to be the symbol of the Church's triumph over adversity. Since its completion in 1893, after forty years of construction, it has come to represent the physical symbol of the LDS Church to its now millions of members as well as to the world. Indeed, the Salt Lake Temple is a monument to a people and its architect.

Brigham Young, the ninth of eleven children, descended from English forebears who settled in New England. His grandfather, Dr. Joseph Young, served as an army surgeon in the French and Indian War. In 1769, he was killed in an accident, leaving his wife with six children. As her economic situation worsened, she was forced to indenture two of her sons, John and Joseph. At sixteen, John took leave of his duties and enlisted under General George Washington to fight in the Revolutionary War. He returned to Hopkinton, Massachusetts, where he completed his obligation of service to a Colonel John Jones and was released from his indenture in 1784. A year later, he married Abigail (Nabby) Howe and for the next sixteen years they struggled in poverty to raise eight children. To improve their circumstances, they moved to Whitingham, Vermont, where five months later, on June 1, 1801, Brigham was born. The poor health of his mother prevented her from nursing, but through the patience of his sister Fanny, who coaxed milk from a reluctant cow, his life was spared.

The harsh winters and unyielding soil prompted the family's move to New York state in search of a more prosperous future. They first settled near Sherburn when Brigham was about eighteen months old. As he matured, he learned the work ethic while farming alongside his father and brothers. The family's destitution also taught him to be thrifty and to sacrifice. Continued economic failure prompted them to relocate farther west in Schuyler County. During this period, at the age of fourteen, Brigham faced his first personal trial—the death of his mother. Her maternal nature had leavened the strictness of a puritan father who allowed his children to walk no more than a half an hour on the Sabbath and forbade them to dance. His mother had instilled in Brigham a strong belief in God and personal redemption that sustained him throughout his life. Her sense of humanity had given him a feeling of personal worth and integrity that allowed him to give freely of himself.

Agonizing over his loss, Brigham abandoned the toils of the farm and its unpleasant memories to seek his own destiny. He moved to nearby Auburn where he expressed his new freedom by attending dances at the local taverns. It was in Auburn that he met his future bride, Miriam Angeline Works.

While in Auburn, Brigham was apprenticed to John C. Jefferies, a skilled chairmaker and painter. After completing his apprenticeship, he settled in Aurelius and became an accomplished chair- and cabinetmaker while branching out into other aspects of the building profession—designing, carpentry, joining, glazing, and painting.

In 1824, soon after he had established himself in his profession, Brigham married Miriam. The two traveled from Fort Byron, first by boat on the Erie Canal and then by coach, to honeymoon in Mendon, where his father and other family members had moved. Impressed with the area and a desire to be close to his family, he moved there in 1829. This move proved to be providential for Brigham's future. The region of western New York was caught up in a revivalist movement in which he and his family were involved. He had long been devoted to the teachings of Christ and had sought to understand the primitive church through his study of the Bible. When rumors began to circulate about "Joe Smith" and his "Gold Bible," Brigham's interest was kindled. His brother Phineas (Phinehas) had received a copy of the Book of Mormon from Samuel Smith, Joseph's brother, and passed it along to his father. Both father and son were soon convinced of its truthfulness. Wishing to test the book's claim for himself, Brigham borrowed a copy from his sister Fanny. Over the next two years, he diligently studied the Book of Mormon, comparing it to the Bible. So convinced did he become of its authenticity that he sought out the missionaries to learn more about the Church. He was subsequently baptized and confirmed a member on April 14, 1832, two years and eight days after the organization of The Church of Jesus Christ of Latter-day Saints.

Though Brigham was satisfied that he had found what he had been searching for, 1832 proved to be a difficult and heartrending year for him. On September 8, Miriam died of tuberculosis, leaving him to care for two young daughters alone. After a few days of introspection, he decided to go to Kirtland, Ohio, to visit Joseph Smith, who moved there from New York because of increasing persecution. He left his children with the wife of his closest friend, Heber C. Kimball. Though he had accepted Joseph Smith as a prophet, seer, and revelator, Brigham had yet to meet him. Their meeting confirmed his belief that Joseph indeed was what he claimed to be—a prophet of God. This conviction made him an unwavering disciple on whom would eventually fall the responsibility as the leader of the Church.

The next year, Joseph Smith asked Brigham and the other Saints to assemble in Kirtland to strengthen the Church and build a temple to the Lord. Soon after their arrival, the members quickly recognized Brigham's talents as a builder; but a call to a leadership position would restrict the time that he could devote either to design or construction work. He was one of 130 men who volunteered in 1834 and embarked on an arduous 1,800-mile journey to rescue the Missouri Saints from mob violence. Though the rescue attempt failed, it proved the loyalty of many within the group who later would be called to important leadership positions in the Church. On February 14, 1835, Brigham Young was ordained to the Council of the Twelve Apostles, a calling which consumed most of his energies. It was also at this time that he met and married Mary Ann Angell, a young convert from Rhode Island who created a secure home environment for Brigham and their children over the next fifteen turbulent years.

On August 19, 1837, after an abbreviated mission in the Eastern states, he returned to Kirtland to challenge disaffected members who were attempting to take over the Church in Joseph Smith's absence. Joseph's decision earlier in the year to keep Brigham in the states rather than permit him to accompany Heber C. Kimball on a mission to England proved to have been prophetic. Brigham demonstrated his maturity of leadership and devotion to the Church by leading a protracted defense of Joseph before his accusers. So fearless and unyielding was his position that the apostates threatened his life. He was forced to flee Kirtland on the night of December 22, nearly a month before Joseph, who had returned from his mission in Canada.

Brigham and Joseph made their way to Missouri after joining company in Indiana. The 900-mile trek during the harsh winter months was grueling, but they were rewarded with a triumphant and affectionate welcome on March 14, 1838. Their joy was short-lived, however, when they learned that some of the members had been unable to endure the hardships of persecution. By August things grew worse when the Missourians called for the Church's expulsion from the state.

Over the next few months, the Saints, and particularly Joseph Smith, suffered from mob violence supported by Governor Lilburn Boggs's extermination order. During this crucial period while the prophet was being held illegally in the Liberty jail, Brigham Young and Heber C. Kimball were given the responsibility of evacuating between six and ten thousand people from Missouri to the neighboring state of Illinois and the Territory of Iowa.

The task of evacuation completed, Brigham Young moved his family to temporary quarters in Quincy, Illinois, while he assisted Joseph Smith, who had just escaped from Missouri, in seeing to the needs of the members. Before he could move his family to a permanent home in Nauvoo, Illinois, with the other Saints, Brigham again was called on a mission—this time to England.

Brigham's mission to England in 1840 had a profound and lasting effect on his life. Returning to his ancestral home, he was captivated by every aspect of his new surroundings. Enchanted by English history, he found it expressed most poignantly in architectural monuments. He especially admired Worcester Cathedral and the monumentality of similar buildings. By his own account and that of his traveling companion, Wilford Woodruff, the buildings that fascinated him most were Westminster Abbey, the Tower of London, and Sir Christopher Wren's St. Paul's Cathedral. He exhibited more than a casual interest in the buildings; he carefully analyzed their style, architectural parts, and historical significance. He spent considerable time appraising Westminster Abbey, and on completion of his visit he purchased an architectural guide to the building. What he saw and experienced became lodged in his memory.

The handful of missionaries were responsible for printing thousands of tracts and other Church publications, including the Book of Mormon. They accounted for 8,000 baptisms in little more than a year and formed a shipping agency to provide the English converts with a means to immigrate to Nauvoo. Their welcomed arrival swelled the depleted ranks of the Saints with badly needed artisans. English accents became common on the streets of Nauvoo.

Brigham returned to Nauvoo in 1841. When not serving the Church on assignments outside of Nauvoo, he built a modest but substantial brick home for his family and provided for their other temporal needs. While in Petersborough, New Hampshire, during his last mission to the Eastern states, he learned of the martyrdom of Joseph Smith and his brother Hyrum in Carthage, Illinois, on June 27, 1844. Brigham immediately returned to Nauvoo. As senior member of the Quorum of the Twelve Apostles, he assumed the leadership of the Church. He had long been prepared by Joseph Smith for this assignment.

Over the next eighteen months he kept the mobs at bay until, with the precision of a modern-day Moses, he directed the evacuation of some 15,000 people from Nauvoo and surrounding settlements beginning on February 4, 1846. He and his company wintered near present-day Omaha, Nebraska, in preparation for the coming season's trek to the Great Basin region. The next spring, he led a vanguard to the valley of the Great Salt Lake, finally arriving on July 24, 1847.

Although President Young's ecclesiastical responsibilities were sufficient for any capable administrator, he also had to direct the settlement of an inhospitable desert and develop a supportive agricultural and industrial base. He organized the Perpetual Emigration Fund to finance the immigration of thousands of Saints to Salt Lake City and oversee their resettlement in California, Nevada, Arizona, Idaho, and Wyoming, forming a network of over 350 outposts and communities. The rapid growth in membership to over 100,000 in forty-seven years was a result of his vigorous missionary program. He sent missionaries to the British Isles, Europe, Canada, the Pacific, and throughout the United States. He accomplished these feats while being harassed by the Federal Government, its appointees, and military detachments, who along with his "gentile enemies" sought to curb his power.

Though he has received appropriate recognition by the present generation for his achievements, Brigham was one of the most misunderstood and therefore maligned persons in his century. His geographical isolation prompted much of the adverse publicity that he received, but his enemies in Salt Lake City also made a point of distorting the truth about his feelings towards the United States and his position on plural marriage. When President Ulysses S. Grant visited Salt Lake City in 1875, he discovered that what he had been told about the deplorable state of the Mormons was not true. He remarked to the territorial governor, George W. Emery, "I have been deceived." Even a skeptical Mark Twain altered his opinion of Brigham Young after he and a delegation from Nevada visited the venerable president in his Beehive House.

> The second day, we made the acquaintance of Mr. Street (since deceased) and put on white shirts and went and paid a state visit to the King (Brigham Young). He seemed a quiet, kindly, easy-mannered, dignified, self-possessed old gentleman of fifty-five or sixty. . . . He was very simply dressed and was just taking off a straw hat as we entered. He talked about Utah, and the Indians, and Nevada, and general American matters and questions, with our secretary and certain government officials who came with us. But he never paid any attention to me, notwithstanding I made several attempts to "draw him out" on federal politics and his high-handed attitude toward Congress. I thought some of the things I said were rather fine. But he merely looked around at me, at distant intervals, something as I have seen a benignant old cat look around to see which kitten was meddling with her tail. By and by I subsided into an indignant silence, and sat until the end, hot and flushed, and execrating him in my heart for an ignorant savage. But he was calm. His conversation with those gentlemen flowed as sweetly and peacefully and musically as any summer brook. When the audience was ended and we were retiring from the presence, he put his hand on my head, beamed down on me in an admiring way and said to my brother, "Ah—your child, I presume? Boy or girl?"

Brigham Young placed great emphasis on education. He saw it as a means to more effectively teach the message of the restored gospel to the nations of the world.

> I wish this people to pay particular attention to the education of their children. If we can do no more, we should give them the facilities of a common education, that when our sons are sent into the world as ministers of salvation and as representatives of the Kingdom of God in the mountains, they can mingle with the best society and intelligibly and sensibly present the principles of truth to mankind, for all truth is the offspring of heaven and is incorporated in the religion which we have embraced. . . . Every accomplishment, every polished grace, every useful attainment in mathematics, music and in all

science and art belong to the Saints, and they should avail themselves as expeditiously as possible of the wealth of knowledge the sciences offer to every diligent and persevering scholar.

He set the example by building a school for his children and having them taught secular truths. He gave each child the opportunity of a higher education for the betterment of himself and the Church. Some attended the local University of Deseret (now the University of Utah) while others, with the encouragement of their father, enrolled in eastern schools. Two of his sons attended the nation's military academies—Annapolis and West Point. Another graduated from the University of Michigan with a fourth from Rensselaer Polytechnic Institute in Troy, New York. They were constantly admonished to improve upon the life of their father, who enjoyed only eleven days of formal education in his seventy-six years.

Though he stressed the importance of secular education, Brigham continually sought balance in his children's schooling. They were taught the principles of the gospel by his example and word. He expected his sons to serve missions for the Church which, as a by-product of their service, would give breadth to their understanding and a love of other people and their cultures. They would further gain from their experiences by observing the latest technological advances of the major industrial countries and bring the information back to improve the standards of their people.

Throughout his life, Brigham Young attracted children because of his gentle nature and genuine concern for them. Among his own children (forty-three lived to maturity) he applied the principles which he taught the saints.

> I will give you a few words with regard to your future lives, that you may have children that are not contentious, not quarrelsome. Always be good-natured yourselves is the first step. Never allow yourselves to become out of temper and get fretful. . . . If the child has in its hand that which it should not have, let the mother or father, or whoever has charge of the child or has the right, take such things from it, and put them away where they belong. Now mother listen to this—never ask a child to give up that which it should not have. Step up kindly and put the article where it belongs. The child will not say anything. A little circumstance took place in Salt Lake City. I had business in a house where I had understood there had been considerable trouble occasionally; and the mother would not let the father speak to the children, to chastise them. I went into the house and talked to the man. The lady came in and sat down. I pretty soon saw a little girl, about two years old, with a tip thimble in her mouth, sucking it. I went up to the girl, took the thimble from her and put it on the mantle shelf. Says I to the mother—"you must not allow the child to have this thing; if it should go into the stomach it will decay." The man looked at me as if he would faint away. He was a large man, but I suppose he

never attempted to say such a thing to his wife in his life. I said it; and the mother was so confounded that she did not say a word; and it would not have done her any good if she had.... I am talking to you of that which I know. I have had an experience in these matters.

He cared for the needs of his children with the wisdom of Solomon. He treated each child as an individual, yet maintained an even course for all that gave them a sense of being and a common direction in their lives. One of his daughters, Susa Young Gates, best appraised her father as a parent.

> The world knows Brigham Young as a statesman and a colonizer; but to his children he was an ideal father, kind to a fault, tender, thoughtful, just and firm. He spoke but once and none were so daring as to disobey. But that his memory is almost worshipped by all who bear his name is an eloquent tribute to his character. None of us feared him; all of us adored him. If the measure of a man's greatness is truly given by Carlyle, as bounded by the number of those who loved him and who were loved by him, then few men are as great as was my father, Brigham Young.

His success as a husband and father should be of equal fame to his achievements as an ecclesiastical leader, colonizer and statesman.

Brigham Young, when not involved with the logistics of the movement and relocation of thousands of people while under pressure from enemies and governmental intervention, was responsible for the solidification of Church government, doctrine, and practice. His longevity, dominant yet persuasive personality, integrity, and practical genius pervaded every aspect of nineteenth-century LDS culture, including architecture.

Brigham Young, because of his concern for education, provided a schoolroom for his children in the Beehive House.

The Beehive House, designed by Truman O. Angell, Sr., was Brigham Young's residence from 1854 to 1877. It represents Young's sense of refined taste and was a fitting residence for the first governor of the Territory of Deseret (Utah) and the President of the LDS Church. Its two-feet-thick stuccoed adobe walls provided warmth in the winter and a cool environment during the summer. Its overall Greek Revival character was enhanced by the delicate veranda and later a covered balcony that acted to shade the interior from the direct rays of the sun. With the lack of native hardwoods and suitable marble, artisans detailed the pine doors and casings to appear as oak and the halls as marble.

Upper left: The front entrance hall and staircase of the Beehive House is where Brigham Young received many dignitaries–Ulysses S. Grant, Mark Twain (Samuel Clemens), Horace Greeley, Ralph Waldo Emerson, and General William T. Sherman, to name a few. Of more importance, the President maintained an open policy for anyone in the Church who sought his counsel. They were to ring the "bell," regardless of the time of day, which was one reason that his bedroom was located immediately to the left of the entrance portal.

Upper right: President Young entertained his guests in what is the most elaborate room in the Beehive House. Located on the second floor along the entire length of the east wall, the parlor or "Long Hall" has been faithfully restored and furnished.

Lower right: The Beehive House kitchen was the center of activity during the daylight hours because of the demands of a large family.

Upper left: Brigham Young purposely located his bedroom at the main entrance of the Beehive House to give immediate access to any who sought his counsel, regardless of the hour.

Lower left: The family bedrooms in the Beehive House were comfortable and well appointed. The large windows provided ample light and ventilation, which Brigham Young felt were necessary for good health.

Brigham Young's large family necessitated the building of a second and larger adobe and sandstone dwelling just west of the Beehive House. Named after the "Couchant Lion" atop the entrance portico, the Lion House (1855-1856) was architecturally unique for the region. Its multiple pitched dormers are reminiscent of fifteenth- and sixteenth-century English urban dwellings. This comes as no surprise, for it was designed in consultation with William Ward, Jr., a young immigrant architect/sculptor/painter from Leicester, England, who was also responsible for the "Couchant Lion."

Upper left: The entrance of the Lion House. *Lower left:* The Garden Room in the northeast corner of the Lion House. The elegantly appointed room served as a sitting room which overlooked the garden area between the Lion and Beehive Houses.

Upper right: The 1875 period room along the west wall of the Lion House. *Lower right:* The front parlor or "Prayer Room" of the Lion House. Here Brigham Young would assemble his large family at about seven o'clock in the evening where the day's events would be discussed, songs sung, and the day concluded with prayer offered by the President.

To determine the suitability of various crops for the region, Brigham Young established an experimental farm on a section of ground a few miles south of Salt Lake City. It also supplied his family with meat, vegetables, and milk which were transported to the Beehive and Lion Houses. Though he did not live on the farm, he did build a large frame and stucco house for other members of his family. Completed in 1863, the carpenters' Gothic cottage was referred to as the "Forest Farm House." Its symmetrical shape, imposing gables, and peripteral veranda gave it a distinctive character. The photo is of the house on its original site before its removal to Old Deseret of Pioneer Trail State Park near the mouth of Emigration Canyon in Salt Lake City.

Upper right: A view of the west sitting room that was reserved for special occasions.

Lower right: A simple but adequate gable bedroom.

During the last years of his life, Brigham Young was afflicted with arthritis. To ease his suffering, he spent the winter months in the warmer climate of St. George, Utah. In 1871, he purchased an adobe vernacular house and had it enlarged by the local architect/builder, Miles Romney, through the addition of a north two-story unit-main entrance hall, staircase, parlor, and bedroom. The new addition gave the house its present "T" shape.

In 1843, Brigham Young designed and built this comfortable brick home in Nauvoo, Illinois. It was a simple design with a central two-story stepped gable block with single-story side wings.

It is often assumed that the medieval character of the Lion House (lower right) was derived from indigenous sources. In part this might be true; however, Brigham Young's visit and exposure to English medieval dwellings similar to the Queen's House within the Tower of London (top right) could very well have served as a source of inspiration. Further, the presence of the English trained architect, William Ward, who is known to have collaborated with Truman O. Angell, Sr., on the Lion House, could likewise have been the source. The importance of this form of architecture to England is reflected in the use of this style through the end of the nineteenth century as seen in the eclectic Victorian buildings in Chester (lower left).

Brigham Young visited Sir Christopher Wren's St. Paul's Cathedral on at least three different occasions to either attend religious services or to explore the many compartments of the second largest ecclesiastical building in the Christian world. The view towards St. Paul's along Ludgate Hill was familiar to Young.

A view into the dome from the nave.

The vaulting of the choir and apse of St. Paul's Cathedral.

Wilford Woodruff, who accompanied Brigham Young on the tour of Worcester Cathedral, recorded the following in his journal: "We visited the ancient noted splendor of the Worcester Cathedral which surpasses anything for splendor and architecture mine eyes ever beheld. It was about 400 feet in length and 800 or 900 years old. It contained many monuments or portraits of persons which were graven out of marble and placed over the tombs or vaults of the ancient Bishops, Lords and Princes, some of which had been there for 700 or 800 years. It is said that some of these monuments with their winding sheets which are carved out of marble are as neatly executed as anything in Europe. Almost everything about this cathedral from top to bottom is carried out in solid marble . . . the whole concept is superior to the architecture of the present generation."

Views of Worcester Cathedral, England

When Brigham Young visited the Tower of London (White Tower), he was attracted to its inherent strength. It is interesting to note the articulation of its walls and the placement of the square towers.

Brigham Young found Westminster Abbey to be of particular interest in terms of its architectural and historical importance. His excitement over the building's Gothic character prompted his purchase of a detailed architectural guide.

Brigham Young probably visited St. Margaret's because of its immediate proximity to Westminster Abbey. Though its present perpendicular style dates from the mid-nineteenth century, it has been an important medieval monument since the fourteenth century.

A short walking distance north of Worcester Cathedral yet visible from the close is the Church of St. Andrew (late 12th - 15th century). It was intact at the time of Brigham Young's tour of the city, but all that now remains is the imposing tower and spire known as "Glover's Needle." The spire was added to the three-stage tower in 1751 by Nathaniel Wilkinson, and that increased its height to over 245 feet, 35 feet higher than the east center tower/spire of the Salt Lake Temple. Like other churches in the region, it no doubt attracted Young's attention.

The west facade of the Nauvoo Temple at Nauvoo, Illinois, as drafted by William Weeks, the architect. This Temple was commenced under direction of Joseph Smith and completed by Brigham Young. By 1848, abandoned by the western migration of the Church, it had been reduced to a pile by mob incendiary and a tornado.

The temple at Kirtland, Ohio, built under the direction of Joseph Smith, was dedicated on March 27, 1836, and became the first "House of The Lord" in modern time. The building was also used for general meetings and housed The School of The Prophets. The eclectic character of the Kirtland Temple is evident on the exterior with the stylistic mix of Gothic, Federal, and Georgian architectural features, while the interior is embellished with Greek Revival motifs.

II

THE SALT LAKE TEMPLE
1853-1893

Brigham Young's carpentry box and monogrammed tools.

THE SALT LAKE TEMPLE
1853-1893

In 1892 an article appeared in the *Deseret News* that questioned whether Truman O. Angell, Sr., was the architect of the Salt Lake Temple. Prior to the Temple's completion in 1893, speculation abounded that William Ward, Truman Angell's former assistant, was responsible for its design. The article was occasioned by Truman's death in 1887 and William's return to Salt Lake City in 1889 to be an instructor in mechanical and architectural drawing at the University of Deseret. His prestigious appointment added credence for those who held the belief that it was he, not Truman Angell, who was responsible for the design of the Salt Lake Temple.

In response to the article, William Ward issued the following statement relative to his position as Truman Angell's assistant:

> I came to Salt Lake in 1850; was first employed as superintendent of the stone cutting department of the public works; afterwards as assistant to Truman O. Angell, the Church architect. In that situation I did not design nor assist in designing the Temple. I did just what I did for any other architect by whom I was employed in a similar capacity subsequently in the Eastern States. It is true that being familiar with stone construction while Mr. Angell's experience had been limited to that of wood, I made out many details of stone work. Only on one occasion did I suggest a feature of the general design: on the first sketches the windows were set near the outside surface of the walls, I recommended that these be set in a considerable distance so the thickness of the walls and the strength of the structure be properly indicated. This was accepted.

Because of this denial, Truman Angell has since been given sole credit for the Temple's design. However, neither should be given this honor; for Brigham Young, as President of The Church of Jesus Christ of Latter-day Saints and final authority on Church architecture, was responsible for it.

> But wait until I dictate and construct it to the best of my ability, and according to the knowledge I possess, with the wisdom God shall give me...

Strengthened by his knowledge as a master carpenter, joiner, and glazier through a broad exposure to some of the world's major architectural monuments, President Young was prepared to begin work on the Salt Lake Temple soon after he arrived in the valley. Unfortunately, he had to abandon his plan immediately because of the departure of his architect, William Weeks.

Even though he was the architect of the Nauvoo Temple and a prominent personality in his own day, William Weeks remains an obscure figure in LDS history. Born at Martha's Vineyard, Massachusetts, on April 11, 1813, to James and Sophronia Weeks, he was trained as a builder by his father. When his family left New England, arriving in Chicago in 1835, he joined his brother Arwin in his architectural practice in South Carolina and Georgia. Following his conversion, William moved to Illinois to be with the Saints.

Prior to Brigham Young's departure from Nauvoo, he made William Weeks part of the vanguard company that would lead the way to the Rocky Mountains. Brigham's intent was to secure William's services as architect of the new temple. Before leaving Nauvoo, Truman Angell, Sr., then supervising carpenter under William Weeks's direction, had been given the responsibility of bringing the Nauvoo Temple to completion in the architect's absence.

His strong attachment to the personality of Joseph Smith, the rigors of the journey, the death of twin daughters, the harshness of the desert wilderness, and the Moses-like rigidity of President Young's organization led William Weeks and three other families to abandon the Salt Lake settlement. Their desertion corresponded with Brigham's return to Winter Quarters to prepare for the next season's migrations. They traveled forty miles north to Goodyear's Settlement (now Ogden, Utah), where they planned to stay the winter.

Well aware that William was a crucial part of the president's plan for the Salt Lake Temple, John Smith, the ecclesiastical and secular authority over the Salt Lake settlement, dispatched Marshal John Van Cott with a letter requesting their return. After the apparent failure of the initial summons, Marshal Van Cott and nine others were sent to bring the Weeks Company back. Embittered, they returned to wait out the winter. In the interim, William sold his architectural instruments and manuals for thirty dollars to finance the purchase of a wagon and a team of mules.

As the Weeks Company made their way east in the spring, they met the President's Company on their way to Salt Lake. In fear of confronting Brigham Young, William fled south but not before he was able to deliver a message informing the president that he and only he was the one qualified to design the new temple and that without him, it could not be built. To this President Young replied:

> . . . tell him he shall not have any peace in his mind until he comes to the valley and makes restitution for the wickedness he has committed and also tell him we can build a temple without his assistance altho Wm. says we cannot.

William Weeks was subsequently excommunicated on October 29, 1848, for his desertion.

The loss of his architect together with the lack of an adequate labor force compelled Brigham Young to delay the construction of the Temple. Over the next four years he kept the project alive by delivering sermons on the commencement, building materials, and general design of the Temple. In 1850, he also replaced William Weeks with Truman O. Angell, Sr., who, after proving himself as Architect of Public Works, was appointed Church Architect.

The ironies of Truman Angell's appointment as Church Architect in 1852 can only be appreciated in the light of crucial events that followed. After months of seemingly endless wanderings through the upper Midwest, William Weeks returned to Utah in 1852. There is little question that his intentions were in part selfish: he had gained old information that an architect had not yet been commissioned to design the Temple. Upon his arrival that summer, however, he was stunned to learn that Truman Angell had already been appointed Church Architect. Instead of making a triumphant entry as the prodigal son to enjoy the full fellowship of the Saints, William Weeks was eventually forced to leave Utah with a company of Saints sent to Southern California in 1856. They settled present-day San Bernardino but were called back to Utah by Brigham Young a year later. Rather than return with them, William Weeks moved to Los Angeles where he died on March 8, 1900.

The bitter winds announced the winter of 1852-53, and accompanying it were the all-too-frequent food shortages. The harshness and deprivations dampened the spirit of the Saints and further delayed the start of the Temple. Sensing how demoralized the Saints were, Brigham Young delivered a timely sermon on February 14 concerning the Temple.

> If you should ask . . . "have you any knowledge concerning this? have you had a revelation from heaven upon it?" I can answer truly it is before me all the time, not only today but it was almost five years ago, when we were on this ground [Temple Block].

His discourse declared a new urgency for the Saints to begin construction of the Temple in the spring. Their discouragement soon turned to optimism. That April, the cornerstones of the Temple were laid and Truman O. Angell, Sr., was sustained by the Church membership as architect.

Truman Angell acknowledged that William Weeks was his superior in architectural skill. But because of his devotion to the Church, Truman—a builder from Providence, Rhode Island—was appointed Temple Architect. Until his death in 1887, except for a period from 1861-1867 when he was forced to retire from the project due to ill health, he was overseer of the Salt Lake Temple project—for thirty-four of the forty years that it was under construction.

Upon Brigham Young's request, Truman Angell commenced with the preliminary drawings for the Temple on January 22, 1853. Obviously encouraged by his work, President Young on February 12 called for an assembly of the people to announce that he would soon show them the appearance of the Temple.

> Concerning this House [Temple], I wish to say if we are prospered we will soon show you the likeness of it, at least upon paper.

The Saints prospered, for on April 6, the cornerstones were laid that marked the beginning of forty years of sacrifice. President Young also spoke of his vision of the Temple.

> I scarcely ever say much about revelations, or visions, but suffice it to say, five years ago last July [1847] I was here, and saw in the Spirit the Temple not ten feet from where we have laid the chief cornerstone. I have not inquired what kind of Temple we should

> build. Why? Because it was presented before me. I have never looked upon this ground, but the vision of it was there. I see it as plainly as if it was in reality before me. Wait until it is done. I will say, however, that it will have six towers, to begin with instead of one.

This was the first time that anyone, except for the president, knew of the general appearance of the Temple. Soon after his address, he visited the architect's office on the Temple Block and sketched his design on a slate and gave a verbal description of the six spires.

Because of the apparent immensity of the task given Truman Angell with his limited skills, Brigham Young introduced him to a man who could assist him with the project. William Ward was a young Englishman born September 2, 1827, in Leicester to William, Sr., and Susannah Ward. His parish record states that he was a gifted child, able to read proficiently at the age of four and competent in mathematics at seven. He was apprenticed at the age of seven to a now-anonymous architect of the English Gothic School. His training in architectural draftsmanship allowed him to cultivate his talents as a painter and sculptor. After completing his architectural training, he was apprenticed to his father in the ancestral trade of masonry, at which he excelled. After his conversion in 1844, he left England for the United States and eventually arrived in Salt Lake City six years later.

Truman Angell immediately introduced William Ward to his responsibilities as an architectural draftsman with the title of assistant architect. The architect rarely mentioned William's talents, but extant drawings show his skill to have been far greater than that of his superior.

Together, the architects were left to particularize President Young's design within the specifics that he gave them. Over the next few months, they completed many of the detailed drawings in preparation for the publication of Brigham's design for the Temple. It appeared on August 17, 1854.

The first description is nearly identical to another published by the architect twenty-seven years later that indicates the thoroughness with which they had resolved the particulars of President Young's design.

In 1855, the major responsibility for interpreting the president's architectural ideas and translating them into finished plans fell to William Ward. He completed the east elevation, a basement floor plan, and a section plan of the east entrance. His final project for the year was a perspective study of the building. Brigham had requested the drawing from the architect; but because he was not competent to render linear projections, he gave the assignment to William. The drawing was so well received that Truman Angell had it varnished, framed, and presented to the president to be hung in his office (the Governor's Office). After William completed the perspective study in August, Brigham Young temporarily removed him from the Temple project to retain his artistic talents through the winter of 1855-56 to paint the Old Endowment House murals.

The importance that Brigham Young attached to English architecture and its influence on his design for the Salt Lake Temple was evident when he called Truman Angell on a mission to England in the spring of 1856 specifically to study the architecture. A blessing given by President Young to the architect prior to his departure illustrates this point.

> . . . you shall have power and means to go from place to place, from country to country, and view the various specimens of architecture that you may desire to see, and you will wonder at the works of the ancients and marvel to see what they have done . . .

In more specific terms, Truman Angell recorded in his diary the objective of his mission.

> I am now making ready for a visit to Europe my ame [sic] will be to visit the works of men a preaching as I go at the same time view the old cathedrals . . . and seek to improve the art of building if the experience can be got more extensively than at home.

Unfortunately, Truman Angell did not possess the same vision as Brigham Young, for he returned with a negative opinion of most of what he saw. His opinion and the design of the Salt Lake Temple were balanced by President Young's and William Ward's understanding and appreciation of English medieval architecture. Though biased against English architecture, Truman Angell had acquired, prior to his mission, an English builder's manual by Peter Nicholson from which he extracted architectural details, building methods, and design concepts for the Temple. Had he not previously finished the design for the exterior of the Temple, Truman might well have taken the journey with greater seriousness.

When Truman Angell departed for his mission in 1856, William Ward assumed his responsibilities as Temple Architect. But suddenly, and without apparent warning, William left his enviable position for the Eastern states some time after July 26, 1856. He did not leave because he was in any way disenchanted with the Church or President Young, but because of resentful feelings towards Truman Angell, who was slow to give proper recognition and respect for those who worked under him.

Truman Angell returned from Europe in 1857, but he did not resume work on the Temple until the late 1860's. The reasons are varied, but began with the War Department's dispatch of an army to Utah Territory. Having received falsified reports of Mormon sedition and treason, President Buchanan sent troops to suppress the imagined rebellion. Upon hearing this, President Young had the footings and foundation of the Temple buried to prevent their possible destruction. As General Albert Sidney Johnston rode through Salt Lake City, he found it deserted and ready to be burned. Colonel John Van Deusen Du Bois, an officer under his command, recorded his impressions after riding through the city.

> The city is beyond my power of description. It is beautiful—even magnificent. Every street is bordered by large trees beneath which on either side run murmuring brooks with

> pebbly bottoms. Not a sign of dirt of any kind to be seen. The houses are surrounded by large gardens now green with summer foliage. All the houses are built of adobe nicely washed with some brown earth, the public buildings large [and] handsomely ornamented surrounded by walls of stone.... But oh how beautiful is this city, not unlike the foliage of plants nourished by corruption. A whitened sepulchre, 'A den of thieves [and] murders' the emigrants say, but to our eyes alone it would seem to be an abode of purity and happiness, a going back to the Golden Age. I say to myself, 'Can it be true?' this story of their crime [and] in spite of the evidence I am dissatisfied.

The army had wintered in the barren cold plain at Fort Bridger, Wyoming. By agreement with President Young the army came through the valley and marched to a site some forty miles southwest, in what is now Cedar Valley. There they built Camp Floyd, which was their home from the summer of 1858 to 1861, when it was abandoned at the outbreak of the Civil War.

Ten months after the departure of Johnston's army on December 18, 1861, President Young ordered that preparations be made to resume construction of the Temple that spring. The previous two seasons had been spent cleaning the dirt from Temple Square to uncover the original sandstone foundation. Within that month, Edward Parry, superintendent of the masons on the project, informed Brigham that the foundation was defective and could not support the weight of the building. The news shocked President Young, who felt a strong sense of urgency about completing the Temple.

The decision of whether to have the defective portions of the foundation footings replaced was difficult because of the costly delay in time and material. But prompted by his desire to have the Temple "last through the millennium," Brigham announced the removal of the defective material on January 1, 1862. The entire structure would be built of "temple granite," actually syenite (similar to granite but with diminished quartzite content). The day of Young's announcement, the workmen began the task of removing the first footings.

Laying the foundation stones was accomplished by no more than eight masons at any one time. The major effort was expended by the stonecutters and shapers at the Temple Block and the stone quarries at the Little Cottonwood Canyon (some eighteen miles southeast of the city). The masons' combined skills brought the walls of the Temple above ground for the first time at the end of the 1867 building season. During this period, the arduous responsibility of expediting the construction work fell upon the shoulders of William H. Folsom, who temporarily replaced Truman Angell as the Church Architect.

William Folsom's arrival in Utah in 1860 came at a critical time because he filled the void left by William Ward. Born in Portsmouth, New Hampshire, on March 25, 1815, he acquired his skills as a builder under the supervision of his father. He was sustained as acting Church Architect in 1861 and retained that position until 1867, when Truman Angell was reinstated after a prolonged illness. During his tenure, Folsom apparently did little more than a stone number and position plan for the foundation wall based on an earlier plan drafted in April 1855 by Truman Angell and William Ward. Both plans included the same inverted arch illustrated by Nicholson.

New drawings for the Temple emerged only after Truman Angell regained his former position and William Folsom was made assistant architect. The first to appear were two drawings in June 1868 (both of the east staircase) derived from an earlier 1855 plan. The June 5 rendering sought to clarify Brigham Young's plan for the inclusion of single canopied sculpture niches at the juncture of the two east doorways and the center tower to receive life-size figures of the martyred Joseph and Hyrum Smith. The June 13 drawing was a stone number and ranking plan.

In 1870, Truman Angell made major revisions in the plans for the exterior of the Temple with removal or alterations of many symbolic motifs. (Brigham Young was responsible for the revisions because of the change in building material from adobe and freestone to granite; granite could not accept the fine detail required by many of the symbols.) The Saturn-stones were eliminated from the upper buttresses and battlements, while the faces of the sun- and moon-stones and the continents that implied the rotation of the earth-stones were either simplified or removed. This simplification was carried into the windows, where sash designs were replaced by sheet glass and tasteful hood mouldings. The changes dramatically reduced the surface ornamentation that detracted from the massive fortress-like strength of the building.

Truman Angell spent most of his time from the late 1860s until his death in 1887 preparing stone number and position plans for the masons. He directed the rest of his energies to the St. George, Manti, and Logan Temples, under construction at the same time as the Salt Lake Temple.

More significant changes in the plans occurred after the death of Brigham Young in 1877. Truman Angell, Sr., in failing health, asked Brigham Young's successor, President John Taylor (1877-87), in a letter, if he could employ his son, Truman O. Angell, Jr., on the Temple project. He wanted to ease his own burden while keeping the Temple construction on schedule. President Taylor agreed to the request.

The first major change in the configuration of Brigham Young's design involved a radical alteration of the Temple's interior arrangement. Truman O. Angell, Jr., while employed as architect of the Logan Temple (1877-84), devised a new interior program to replace the original hall design patterned on the Nauvoo Temple. The new arrangement allowed easier access and a more logical movement of temple patrons from room to room and floor to floor. Truman Angell, Jr., wrote President John Taylor, asking his permission to use his design proposal in the Logan Temple.

> Our late President Young said that it was not required that temples be alike, neither in the interior or exterior design and construction. I have the building planned for greater convenience but can easily change the location of said rooms if you see fit to order it so.

Fifteen days later, the president enthusiastically approved the plan.

After the completion of the Logan Temple in 1884, the son returned to Salt Lake City to once again assist his father with the Salt Lake Temple. Truman Angell, Jr., promptly took the initiative by first submitting to President Taylor a proposal to construct the spires of granite rather than wood with a metal sheathing. Then on April 28, 1885, he submitted a series of revised interior plans based on his Logan designs. With the plans, he sent the following letter of explanation.

> I herewith submit two sets of drawings pertaining to the interior construction and arrangement of the Salt Lake Temple; the first set (the original) accepted by the late President Brigham Young, comprised the following; first, the building would contain a mass of interior columns; second, it would have two large assembly rooms with two stands in each thereby, except the Garden, which would be out south of the Temple about seventy yards; third, there would be four outside entrances on the sides to the basement difficult to protect from storms; fourth, it has four tiers of rooms lighted by elliptical windows, thirty-two in number.... The other set is a proposition drawn up from a standpoint of experience and progression and has the following strong points; first, columns are entirely done away with except under the gallery where absolutely necessary and then only four inch iron; second, but one large assembly room with stands in each end and galleries instead of tiers of rooms; third, but one outside entrance to basement and that connected with a building one hundred feet to the north, by an underground passage; fourth, but sixteen small rooms lighted by elliptical windows; fifth, three hundred persons could go through in one day with convenience, while the first plan would only accommodate less than half that number clumsily.

He had previously shown his father this proposal and included his name on the plan. But Truman Angell, Sr., hearing of his son's attempt to gain approval for its implementation, immediately wrote President Taylor to persuade him not to change Brigham Young's plan.

> Shortly after our arrival here President Brigham Young wanted me to start on the temple design of six towers; three on the east and three on the west: both sets connected to the main body of the building. The house was designed about 34 years ago; and as I got the plans ready I took them to President Young and he approved them, both exterior and interior. The outer parts are now up except topping out of towers.
>
> All we knew of temples then was what we had received through President Smith....
>
> President Young said all along he meant to have a real garden and a house suitable to the

> accommodation of the same in connection within (Salt Lake) Temple. This he urged on my mind for quarter of a century. It seems to me to alter the plans now would make a bad thing of the house: but I should think the plans as approved all along until now better continue. I know it will do if you consent to the same. The seating capacity to the large rooms are equal to eight tons of people and to take out the piers and stays as shown in the transverse plan it seems to one should not be done but be carried out as there set forth.

Apparently, Truman Angell, Jr., received a favorable response from the President to his new interior arrangement as he did on the Logan Temple. However, he was less successful in his effort to alter the spires.

When Wilford Woodruff (1887-98) succeeded John Taylor as Church president, Truman Angell, Jr., again seized the opportunity to present his own plan regarding the spires.

> Three years ago last June [1884] I suggested to our late president Taylor the propriety of completing the temple towers of stone instead of topping them with wood, after holding the matter under advisement for several months he concluded to favor wood according to the original designs, but the question since has almost ever been on my mind, and I feel impelled to bring the matter up again for consideration. I am very enthusiastic in favor of stone instead of wood and very respectfully beg to submit the question.

President Woodruff, in a letter to the son dated October 4, 1887, agreed to his plan. But the father, learning of the decision, sent the president a letter pointedly asking him to reverse his action. Though sympathetic to his view, the President refused the request. On October 16, after working at his architectural office on Temple Square, Truman O. Angell, Sr., returned home where he died late that evening from multiple causes, complicated by a severe cold.

The years following Angell's death were difficult. Work on the Temple was complicated by the Federal Government's enforcement of the Edmunds-Tucker Act of 1887. The Act sought to disincorporate the Church because of the plural marriage issue. A provision of the Act provided for the escheatment of all Church property with an assessed value greater than $50,000. The Church did work out an agreement, however, where they had to pay a monthly rent of only one dollar to the court-appointed receiver to utilize the facilities on the Temple Block, including the Salt Lake Temple. Under this arrangement, work on the Temple continued.

Within a few months after the death of Truman O. Angell, Sr., Joseph Don Carlos Young was appointed to be his successor. By the spring of 1888, he was already revising Angell's plans for the interior of the building. It was appropriate that one of Brigham Young's sons would be responsible for the completion of the Temple. Don Carlos' appointment marked a new era in which the Church would have available academically trained architects. Though he received his degree in engineering from Rensselaer Polytechnic Institute at

Troy, New York, in 1879, he had always been interested in architecture. As the temple architect, he supervised the completion of the granite spires. He did make changes in the original plan, primarily to accommodate the suspension system for Cyrus E. Dallin's nearly thirteen-foot gold-leaf statue of angel Moroni.

Don Carlos' major contribution was redesigning Truman Angell, Jr.'s plans for the interior of the Temple while maintaining his predecessor's basic layout and movement. He altered the configuration of the basement floor by centering the baptismal font in a large room with dressing areas to the north and south. He also straightened and enlarged the access corridor, brought the Garden Room from the second floor to the basement, and shifted the orientation of the two endowment rooms (Creation and Garden Rooms) to the south. He revised the second floor by resolving the access corridor and dividing the remaining area into quadrant rooms arranged in a counter-clockwise movement. The southeast quadrant was specifically subdivided into sealing rooms, sealing room annex, and the Holy of Holies. He completely altered the arrangement of rooms on the third or Council Room floor. The change was necessary to accommodate the high ceilings of the Celestial Room and the Holy of Holies that pushed into the third from the second floor. His plans for the fourth or Assembly Room floor involved a lyrical integration of the galleries with the terraced priesthood pulpits at either end. The result was a more aesthetically pleasing and unified design.

Like his father, Don Carlos influenced his generation of Church architecture. He introduced concepts for the present system of standard planning, with a central aim to minimize design and construction costs. Before his death on October 19, 1938, he did much to change the character and direction of architecture in Salt Lake City and in the surrounding regions.

Dedicated on April 6, 1893, exactly forty years after the laying of the cornerstones, the Salt Lake Temple stands as a monument to remind the present generation of Brigham Young's architectural vision, the sacrifice of those who built the Temple, and the Faith that brought them to the valley of the Great Salt Lake.

THE MEN WHO INSPIRED AND LAID THE TECHNICAL GROUNDWORK FOR THE SALT LAKE TEMPLE

Brigham Young sketched his design concept for the Salt Lake Temple on an office slate for his architect and assistant and then asked them to refine it. The design proposal represented the sum total of his personal experiences as a joiner-glazier and an astute observer of architecture. He then synthesized his experiences with an encompassing theosophical perspective to arrive at a visual statement of Mormon belief.

Truman Osborn Angell, Sr., was appointed architect of the Salt Lake Temple in 1853 by his brother-in-law, Brigham Young. Except for a brief period between 1861-67, he held that position until his death in 1887, when the responsibility passed to his son Truman Osborn Angell, Jr. His son had assisted him as draftsman on the Temple since 1877. The son was replaced by Joseph Don Carlos Young, who completed the Temple in 1893.

The architecture and sculpture studio of William Ward, Jr., was located just north of the Temple Block. He received numerous commissions which included the Utah State Seal in the Washington Monument, the "Couchant Lion" atop the entrance portico of Brigham Young's Lion House, and numerous gravestones in the Salt Lake City Cemetery. He also painted the landscape murals in the Endowment House on the Temple Block.

William Ward, Jr., a young English convert, was Truman O. Angell, Sr.'s assistant during the design phase of the Salt Lake Temple. His broad training and abilities exceeded those of the architect, to the point that a year before the Temple's completion, it was rumored by some that William Ward, not Truman Angell, was responsible for the Temple's design. The Ward family still holds to this belief. William died in Council Bluffs, Iowa, on January 4, 1893.

William H. Folsom was a builder/architect of ability. When in Omaha, Nebraska, he soon opened an architect's office on Main Street and began to apply his trade. Throughout his career, he was responsible for a number of important buildings in Utah–Salt Lake Theatre, Amussen Building, ZCMI, Gardo House, and Provo Tabernacle. His greatest architectural achievement was the Manti Temple (1875-88), the most aesthetically pleasing of Brigham Young's four temples.

Joseph Don Carlos Young was born on May 6, 1855, the fourth child of Brigham and Emily Dow Partridge Young. Family tradition and documents support the idea that he was responsible for the design of the granite spires and much of the interior of the Salt Lake Temple.

Temple Square as it appeared in 1893.

Left: One of Truman O. Angell, Sr.'s original 1853 proposals for the recessed windows of the Temple.

Lower left, upper right: Truman O. Angell, Sr.'s study for the battlements of the Salt Lake Temple is reminiscent of those on Peter Nicholson's Seat of Henry Monteith, Esq. The entrance tower and flanking bay window pavilions of Nicholson's drawing also bear a striking resemblance to the east and west facades of the Salt Lake Temple. Truman O. Angell, Sr., made use of Nicholson's volume, The Practical Builder, *to refine Brigham Young's design proposal.*

Opposite lower left: The 1854 south elevation of the Salt Lake Temple. Notice the oval window in the left corner tower compared to the finished building.

Opposite lower right: The 1855 east elevation of the Salt Lake Temple by William Ward.

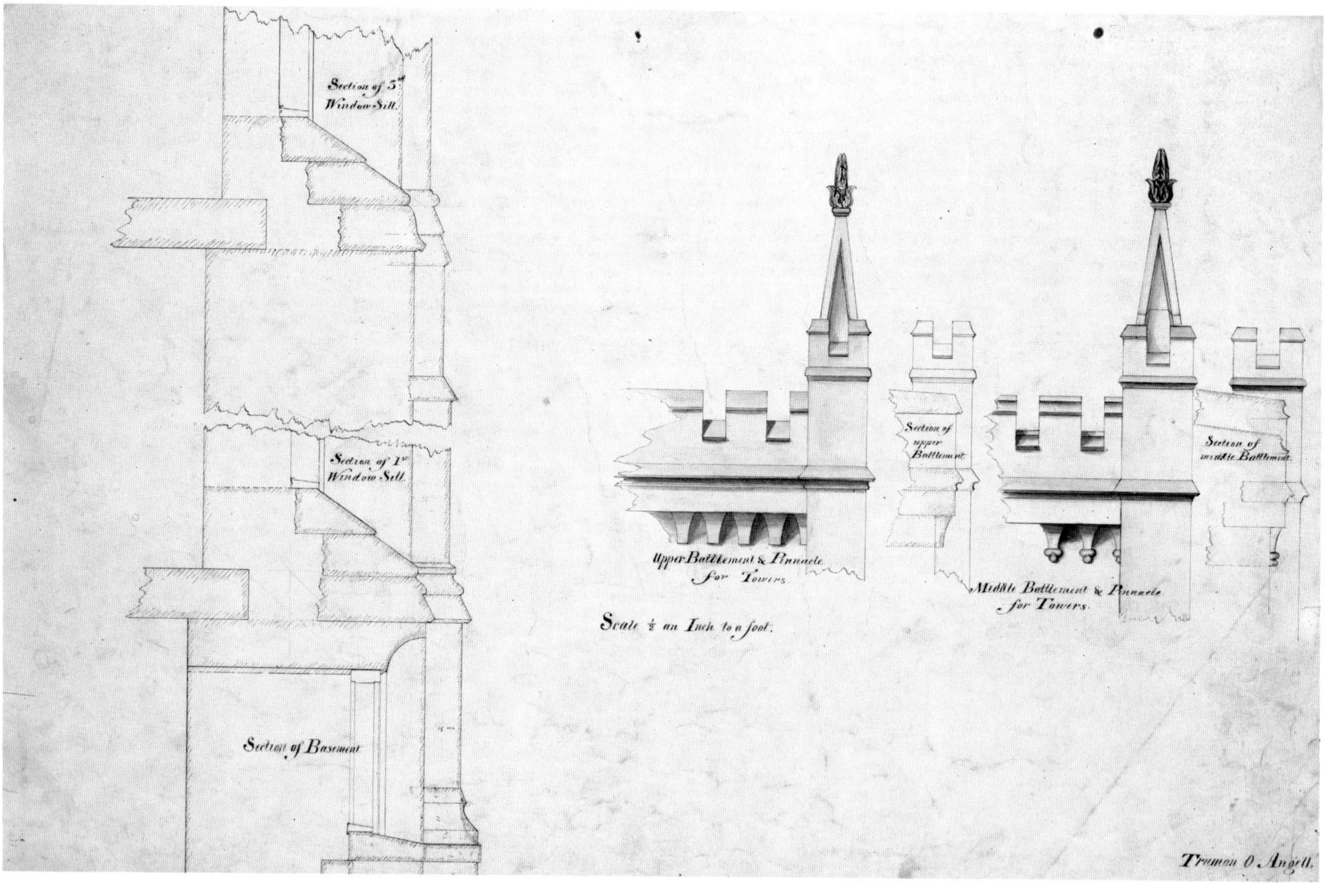

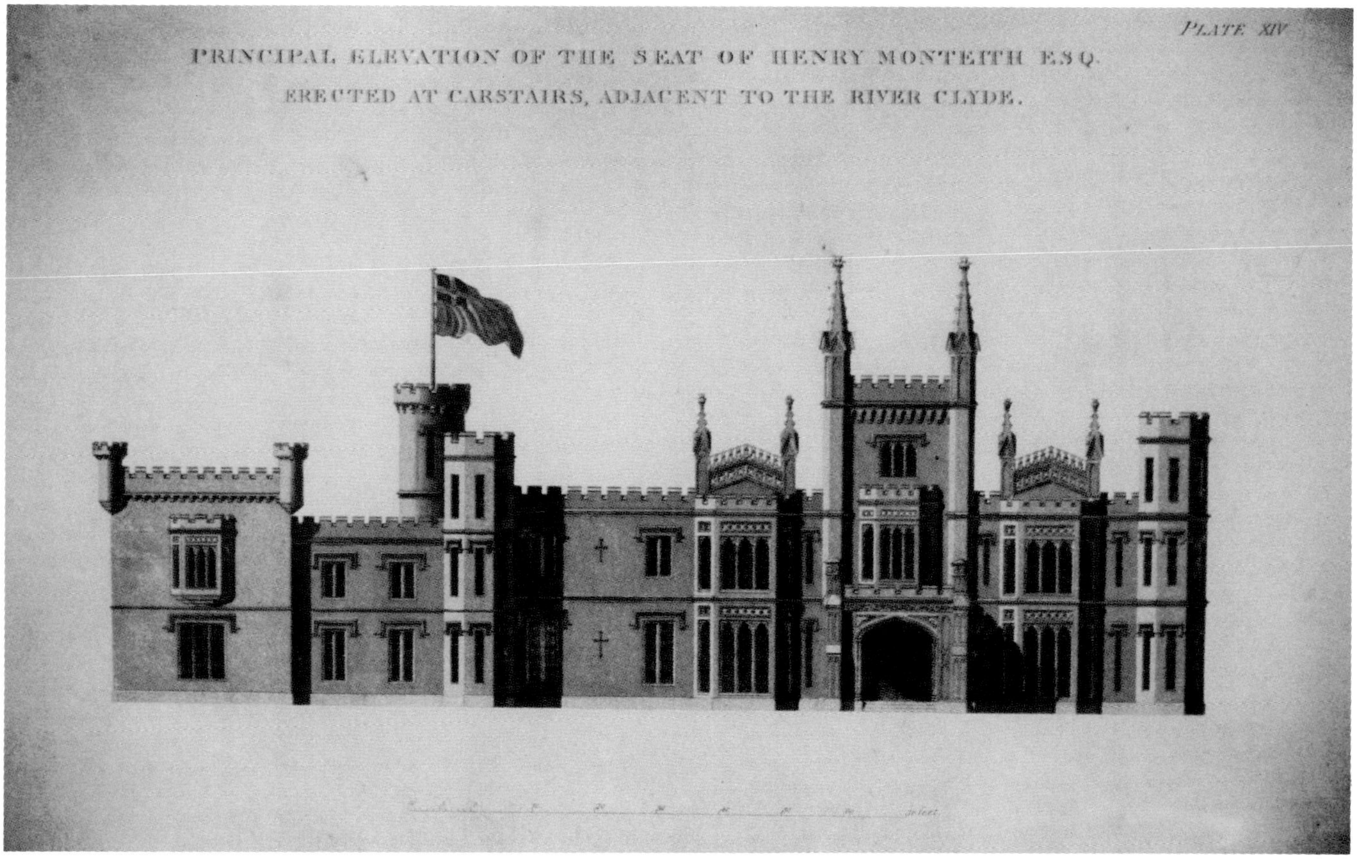

PLATE XIV
PRINCIPAL ELEVATION OF THE SEAT OF HENRY MONTEITH ESQ.
ERECTED AT CARSTAIRS, ADJACENT TO THE RIVER CLYDE.

TEMPLE.

TEMPLE.

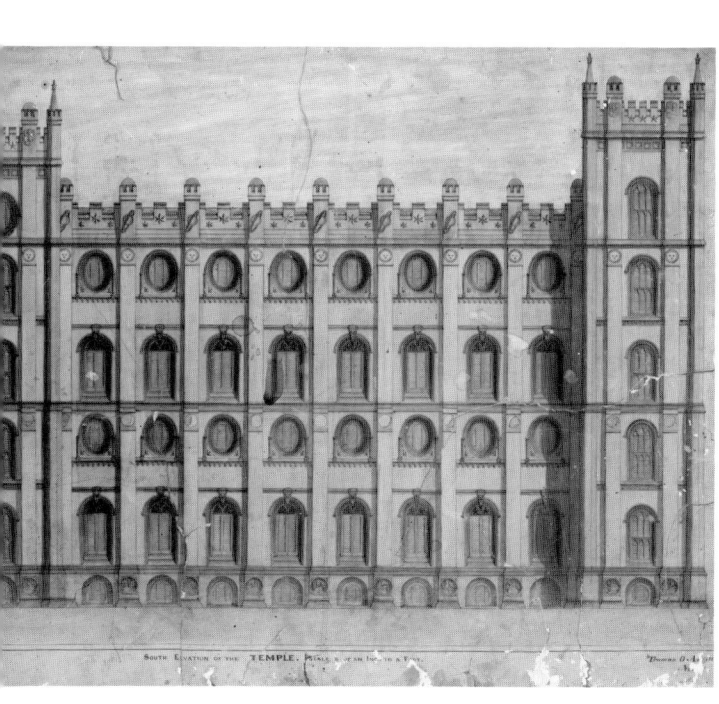

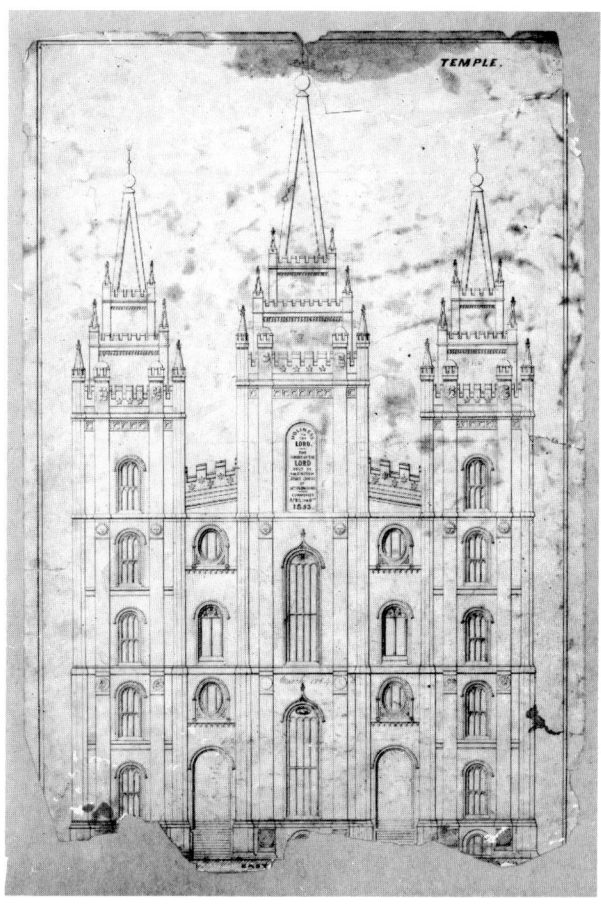

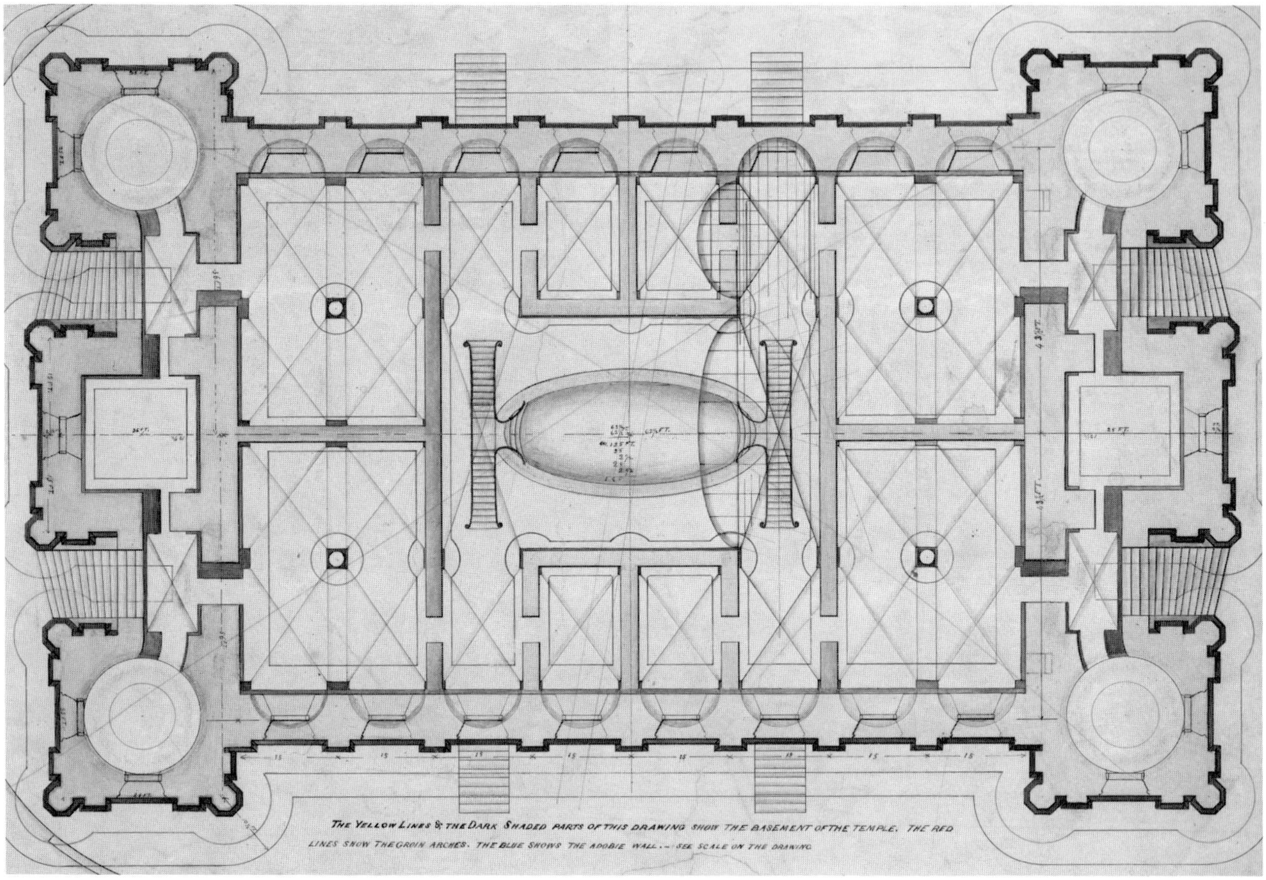

Upper: The plan for the basement floor drafted by William Ward in 1854.

Right: Truman O. Angell, Sr.'s response to Brigham Young's request for a Garden Room Annex off the basement floor. Its three-wall southern exposure would have permitted the planting of an interior garden that would have given the desired atmosphere associated with the activities of the room.

Opposite: The structure application of the inverted arch is apparent in William Ward's 1855 plan of the east entrance staircase (lower) and William Folsom's 1862 stone placement and ranking plan for the foundation wall (upper).

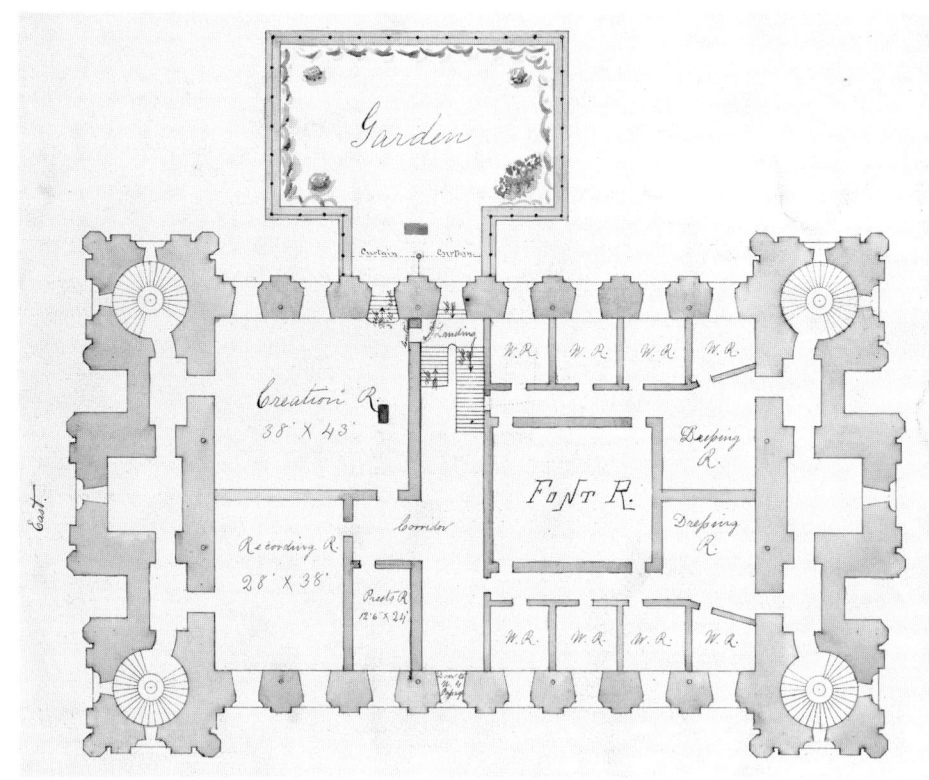

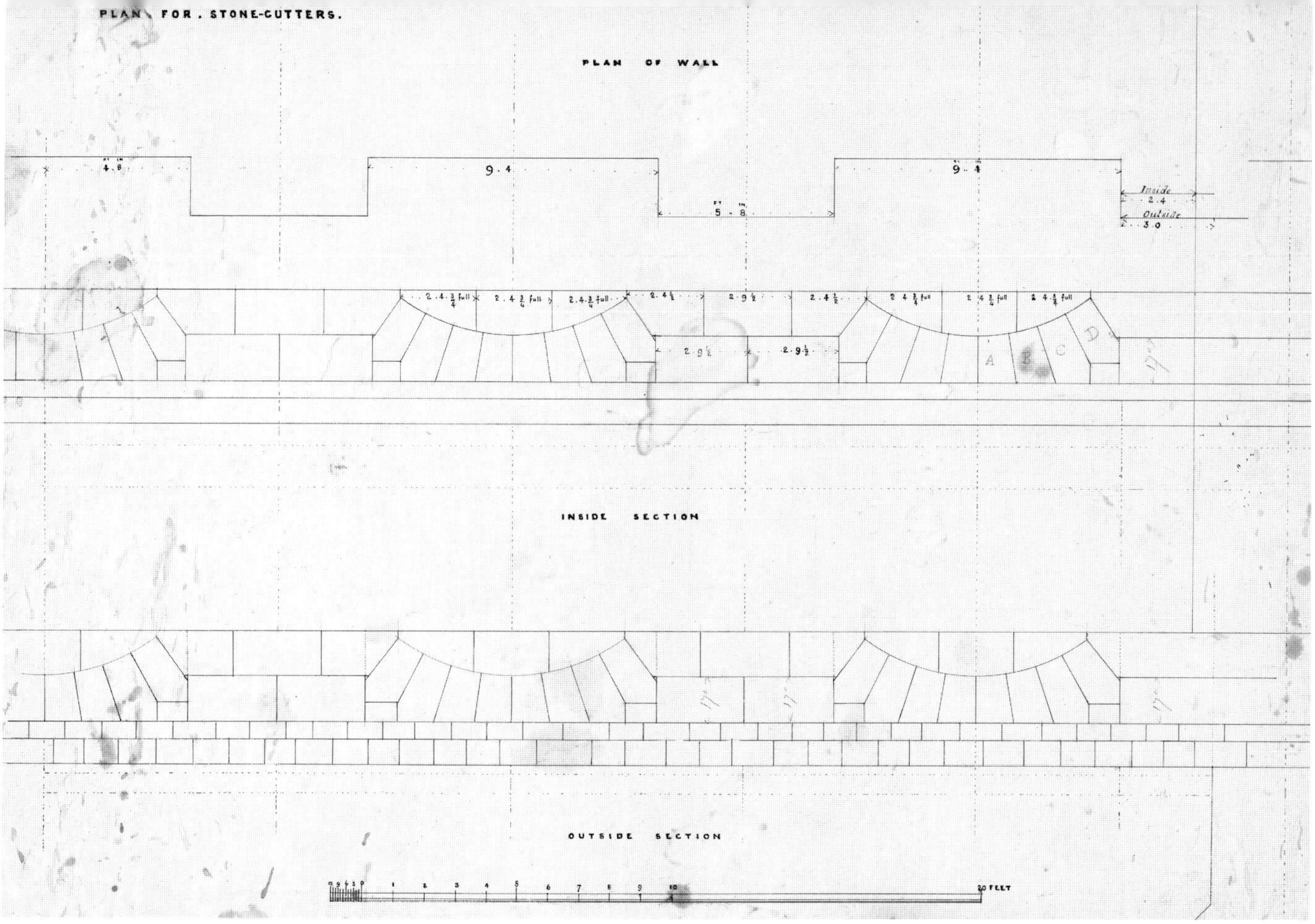
PLAN . FOR . STONE-CUTTERS.
PLAN OF WALL
4.8
9.4
5.8
9.4
Inside
2.4
Outside
3.0
INSIDE SECTION
OUTSIDE SECTION
20 FEET

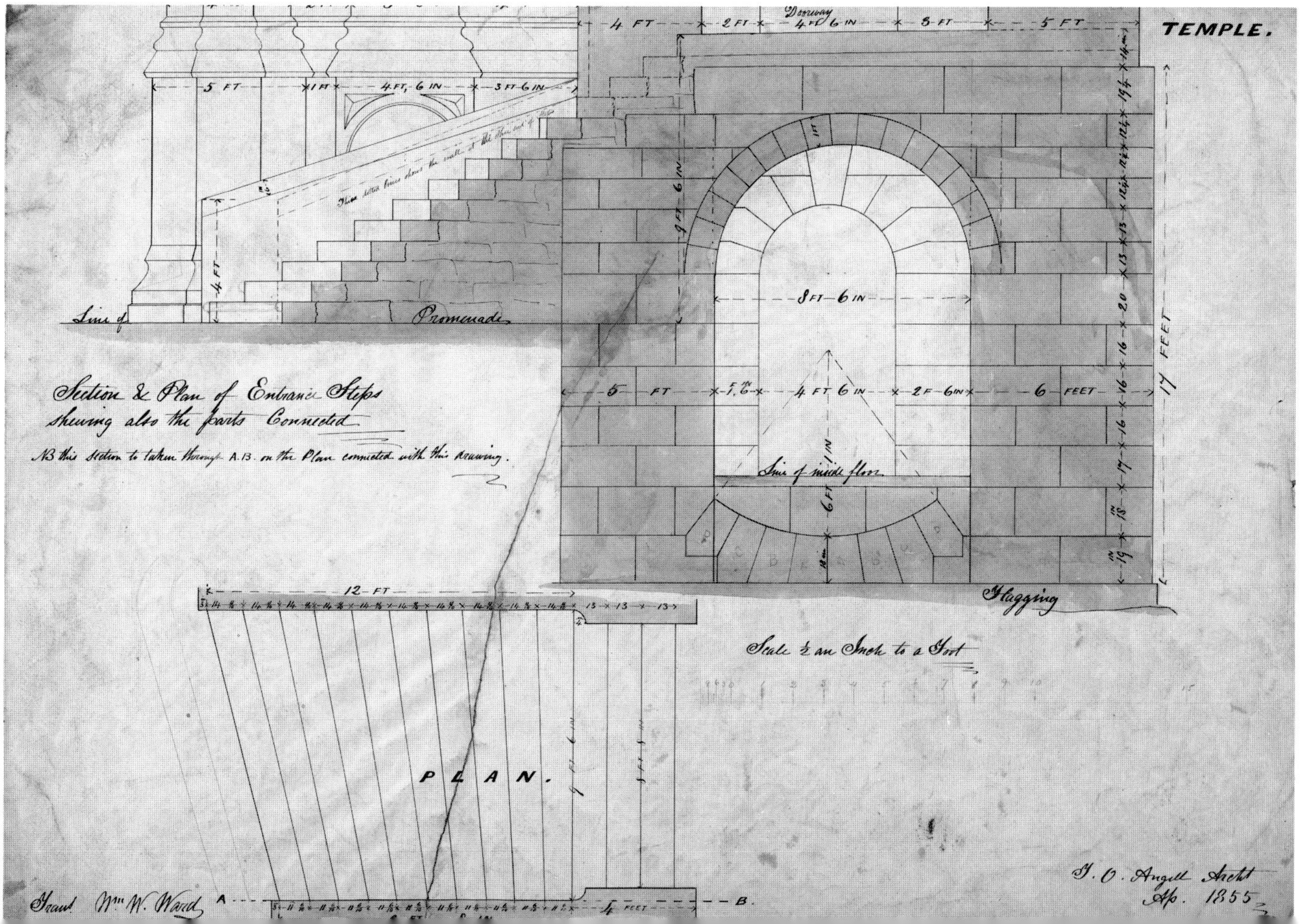
TEMPLE.
Doorway
Line of Promenade
Section & Plan of Entrance Steps
shewing also the parts Connected
NB this section is taken through A.B. on the Plan connected with this drawing.
Line of inside floor
Flagging
17 FEET
12 FT
Scale ½ an Inch to a Foot
PLAN.
Grant. Wm W. Ward
J. O. Angell Archt
Ap. 1855

Above: The print of the Salt Lake Temple from an engraving made in England from a daguerreotype of William Ward's perspective study. The daguerreotype was taken to England by Truman O. Angell, Sr., in 1856.

Right: William Ward was responsible for the recessed windows of the Salt Lake Temple. The change from Truman O. Angell, Sr.'s proposal for flush exterior mounted windows preserved the inherent fortress-like strength of the building which was consistent with Brigham Young's feelings that it would stand for a thousand years.

Far right: Truman O. Angell, Sr.'s June 1868 plan of the east entrance staircase was the first to exhibit the sculpture niche. The sculpture niches on either side of the east and west central towers go unnoticed by the casual observer. Until 1911, the eastern niches housed the bronze historical figures of Joseph and Hyrum Smith by Mahonri M. Young, a grandson of Brigham Young.

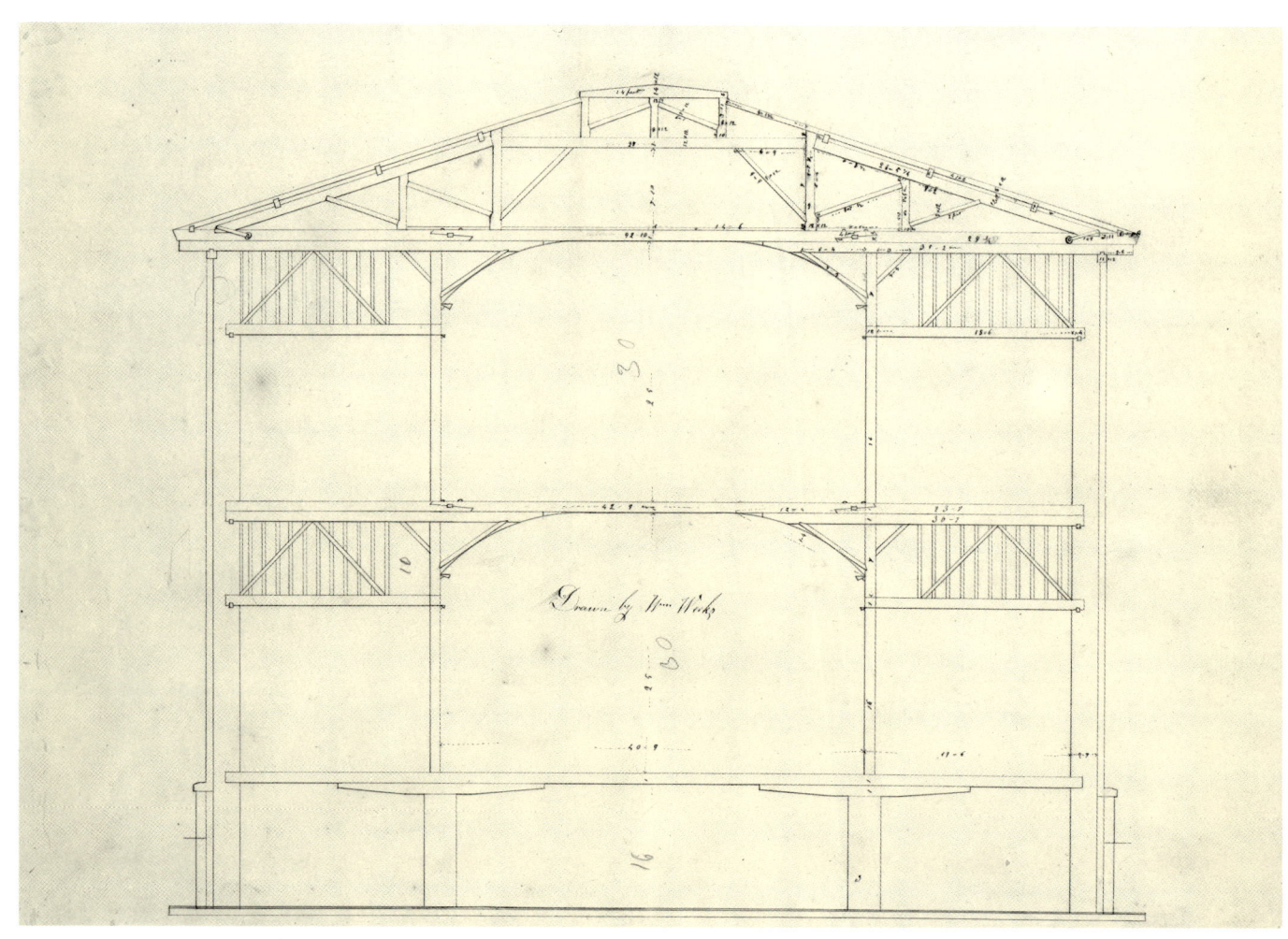

Transverse section of the Nauvoo Temple by William Weeks.

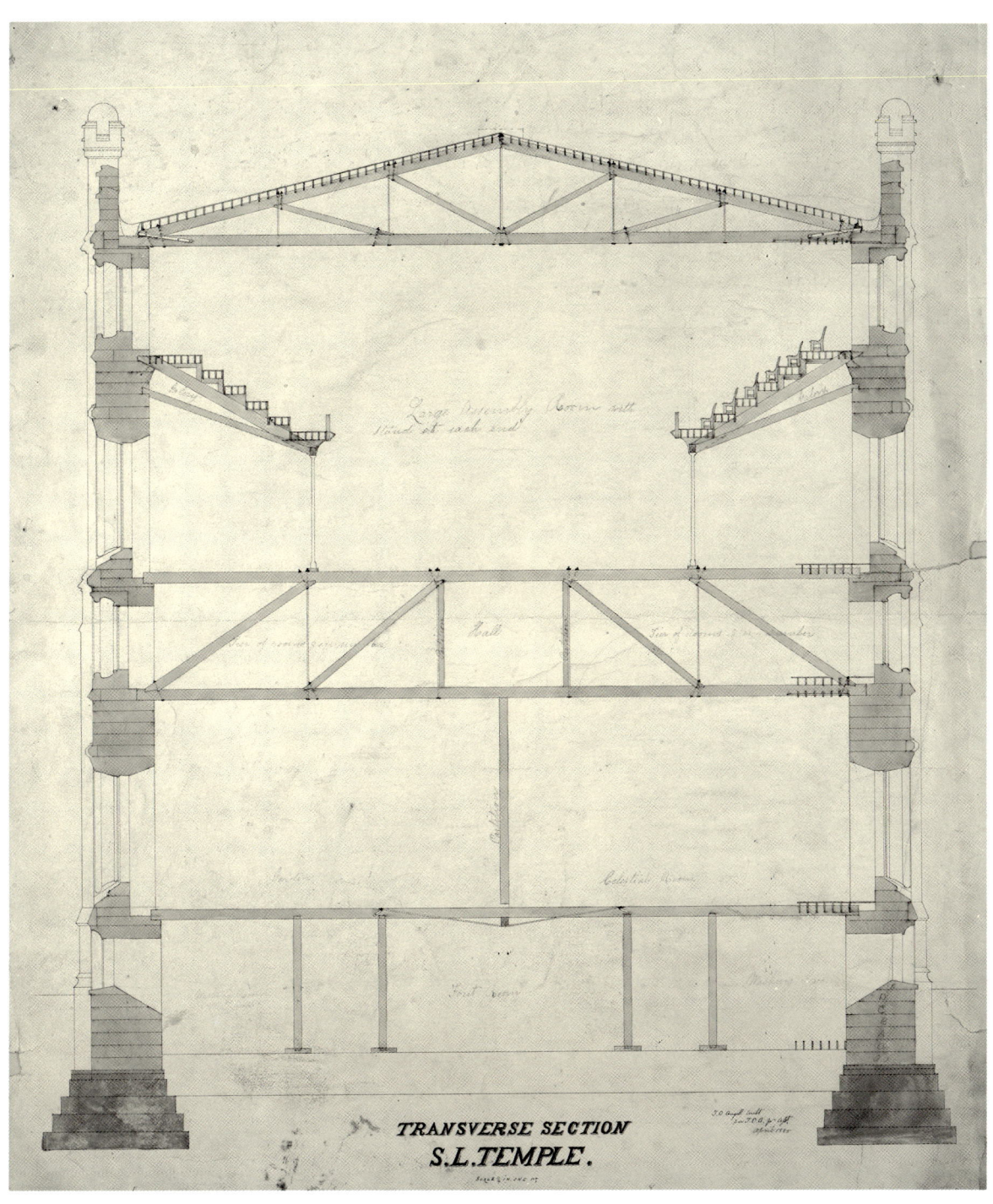

The original transverse section of the Salt Lake Temple drafted by Truman O. Angell, Jr., for his father. It was patterned on William Weeks's design for the Nauvoo Temple.

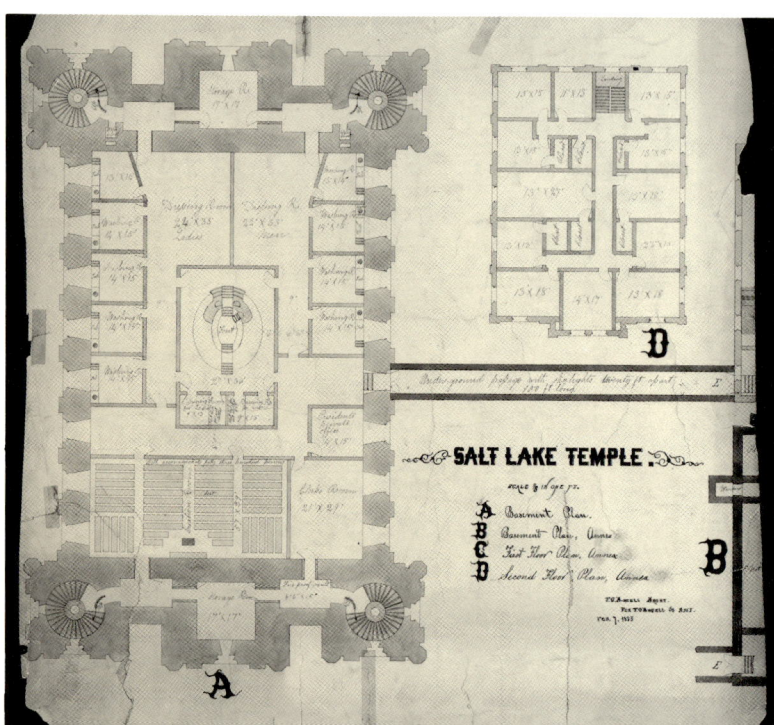

Truman O. Angell, Jr.'s February 7, 1885, plan for the basement floor that he submitted to President John Taylor for his approval. At one time, it included plans for a two-story annex with a basement that was connected to the Temple by an underground corridor (B, C, and D).

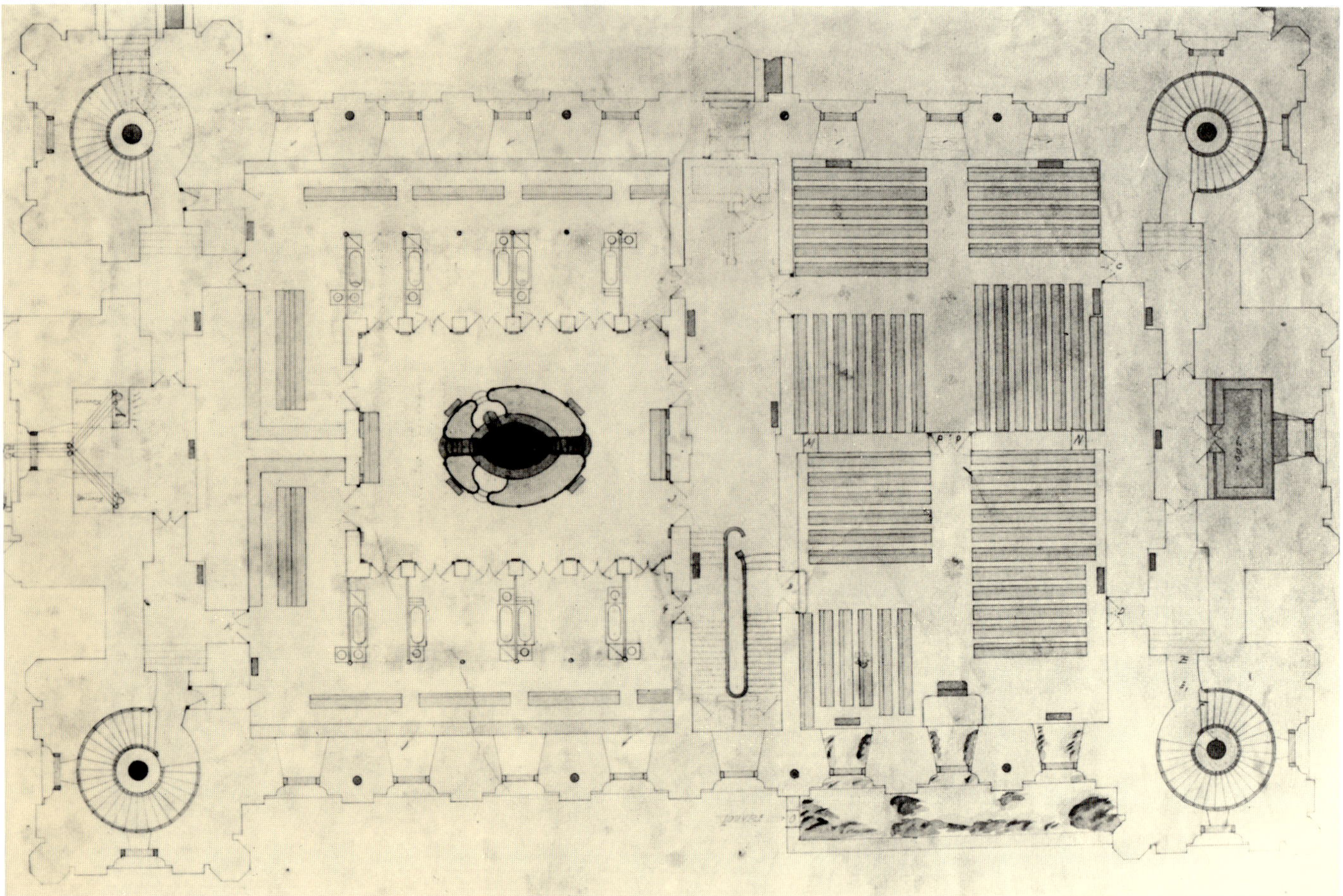

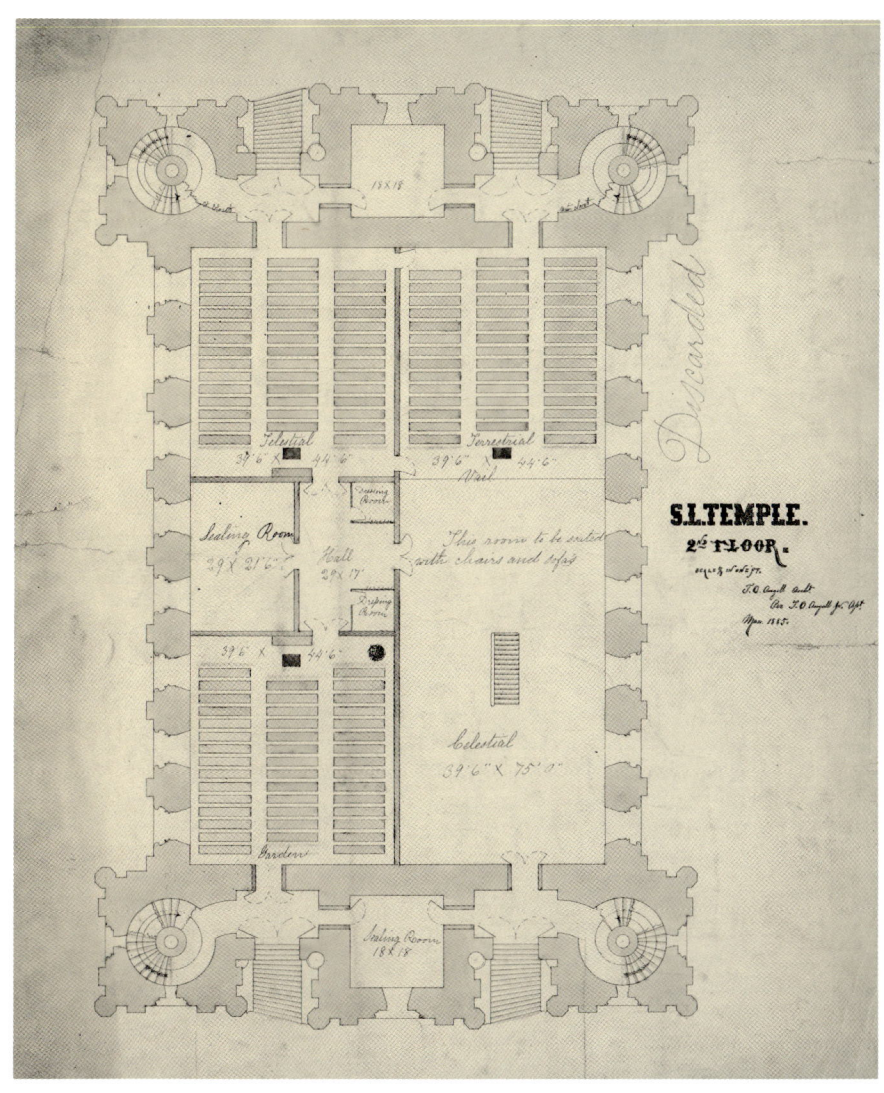

Truman O. Angell, Jr.'s March 1885 plan for the second or Endowment/Sealing Room floor that he submitted to President John Taylor. It is very similar to the present floor plan by Joseph Don Carlos Young.

ANGEL MORONI ANCHORAGE
SALT LAKE TEMPLE

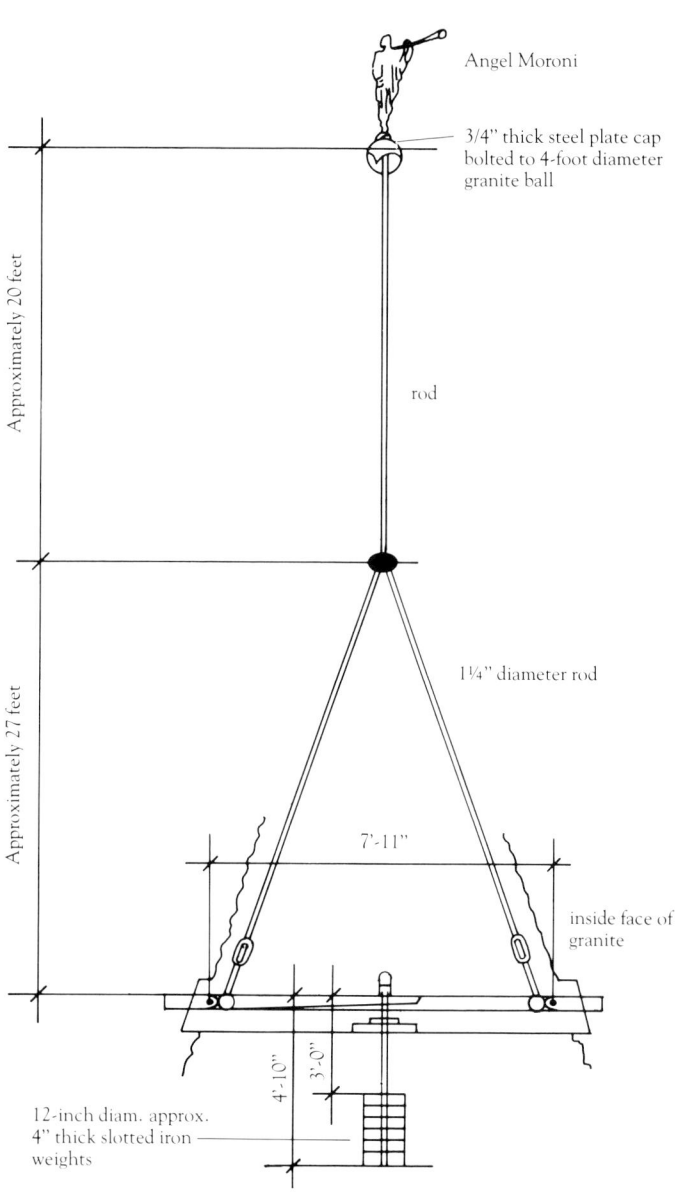

The unique suspension system designed to eliminate the deflection of the twenty-five-foot high 1,500-pound copper statue of Angel Moroni by Cyrus E. Dallin.

ANGEL MORONI ANCHORAGE LEVER ARM DETAIL
SALT LAKE TEMPLE

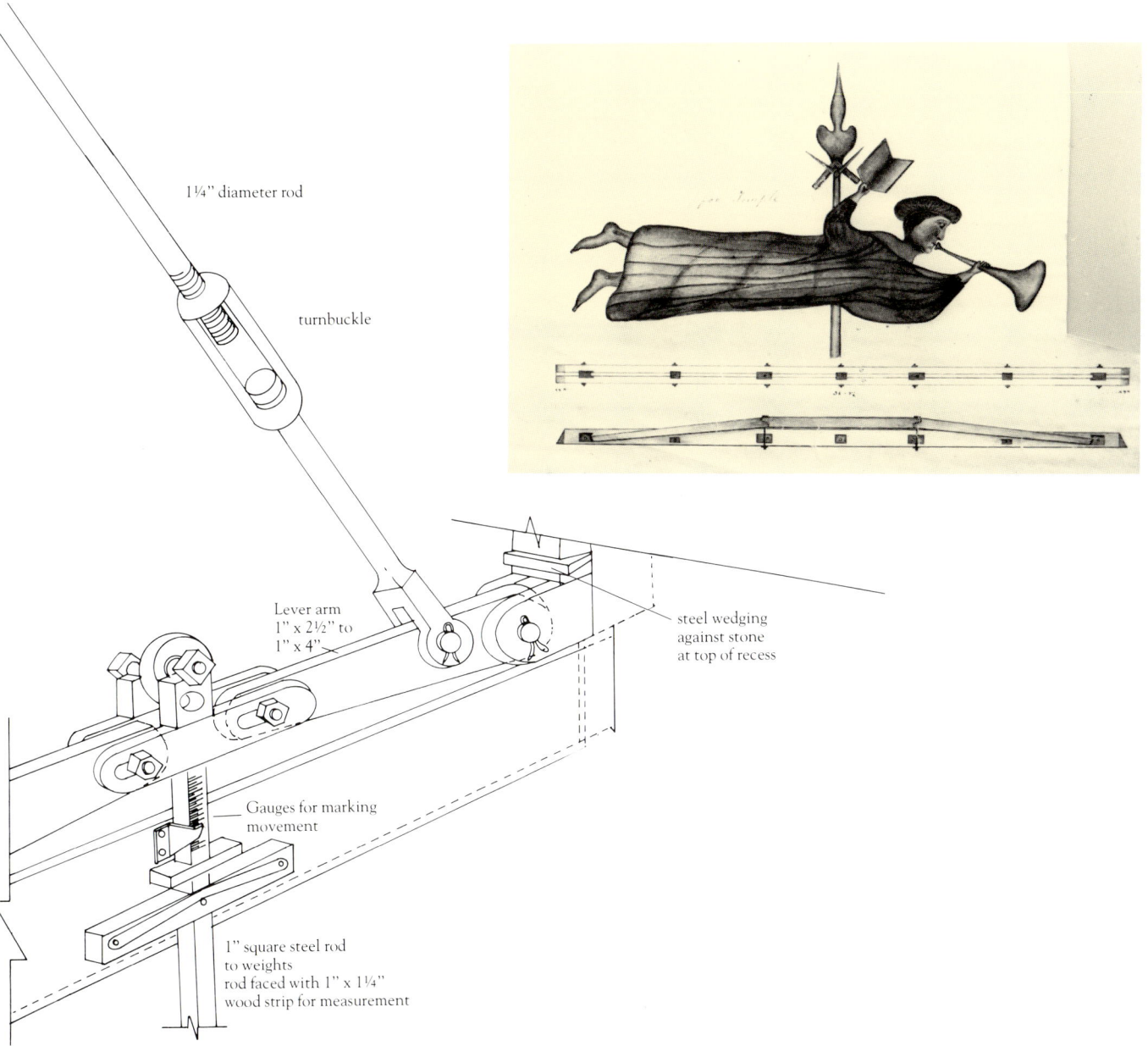

Cyrus E. Dallin's classical figure of Angel Moroni replaced the proposed in-flight figure by Truman O. Angell, Sr., which he patterned on the weather vane-type by William Weeks on the Nauvoo Temple. The stylistic change reflects the redirection of the LDS Church from a provincial to a world perspective.

Below: Truman O. Angell, Jr.'s November 1886 plan for the third or Council Room floor.

Upper right and lower right: The January 1887 plan for the fourth or Assembly Room floor by Truman O. Angell, Jr. When compared to the plan by Joseph Don Carlos Young, it exhibits an obvious dependence on the earlier Kirtland and Nauvoo Temples.

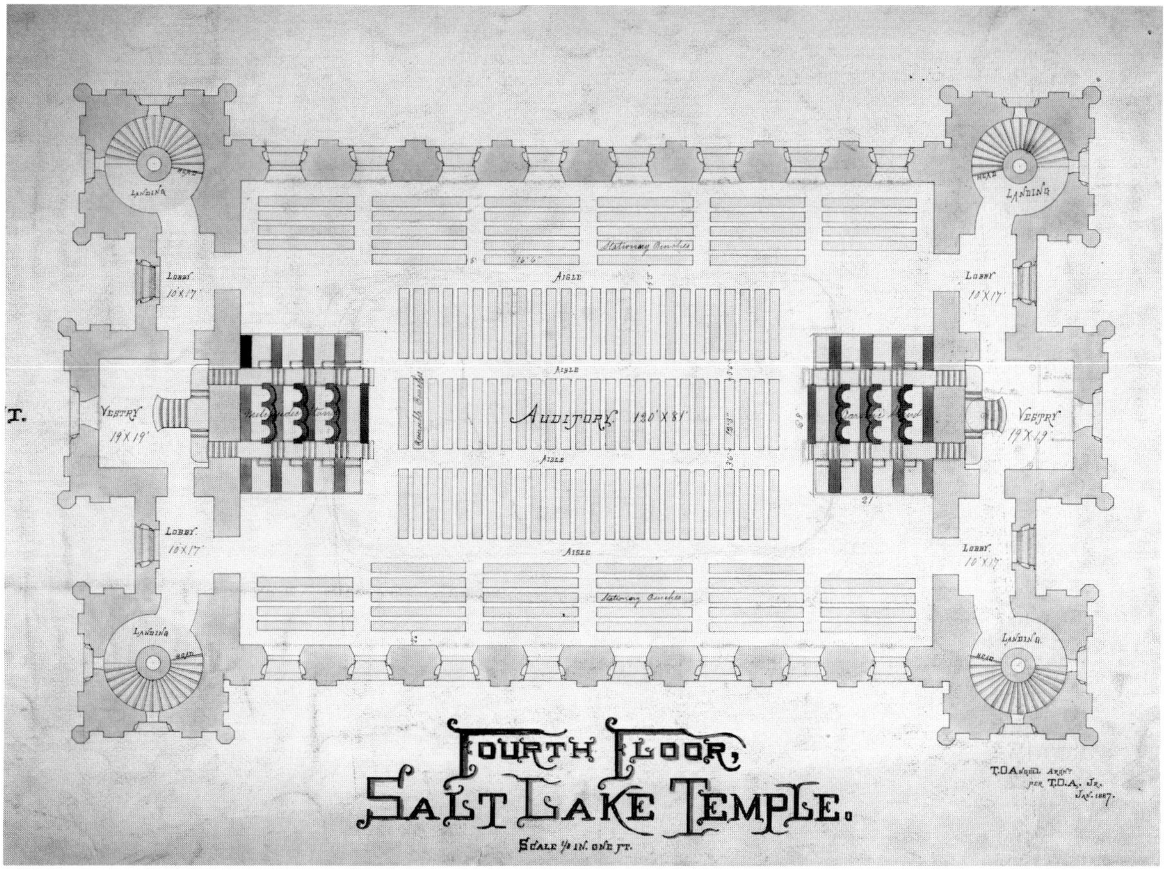
LANDING
LOBBY 10'X17'
VESTRY 19'X19'
AISLE
AUDITORY 120'X81'
Stationary Benches
FOURTH FLOOR,
SALT LAKE TEMPLE.
SCALE 1/8 IN. ONE FT.
T.O. Angell Archt
per T.O.A. Jr.
Jan. 1887.

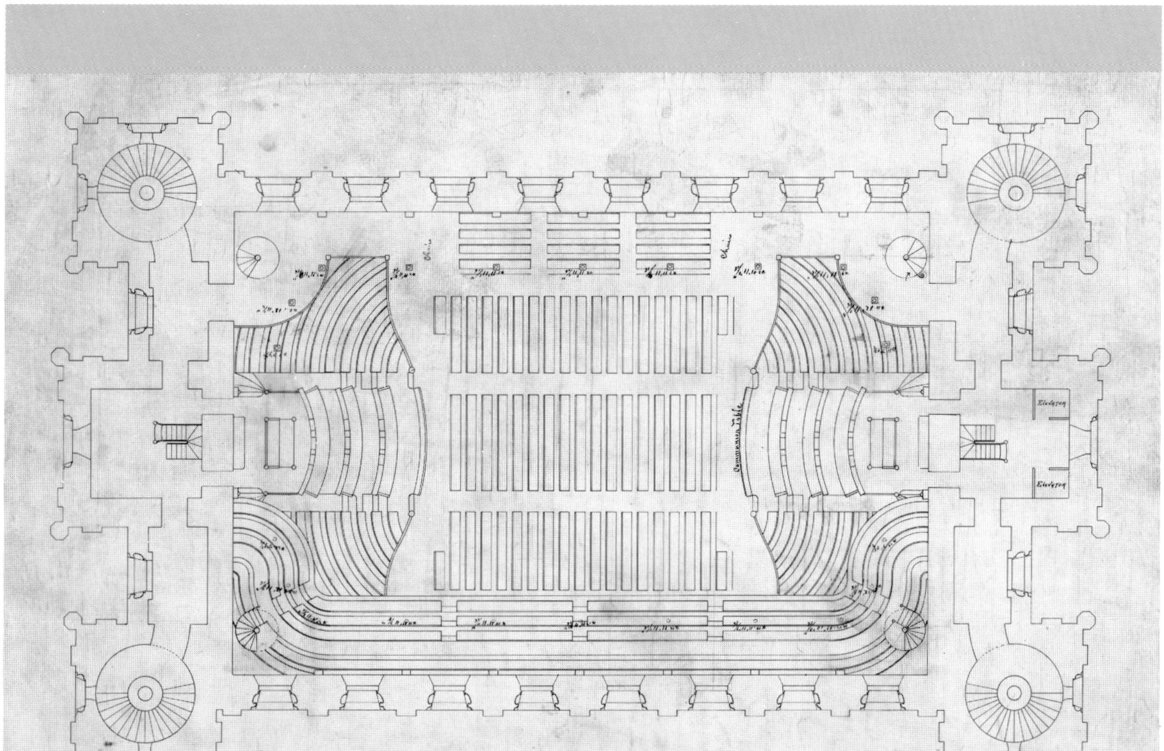
Elevator
Communion Table

Truman O. Angell, Sr.'s original September 1884 plan for wood spires with a protective metal sheathing was replaced by his son's November 1887 plan for granite spires.

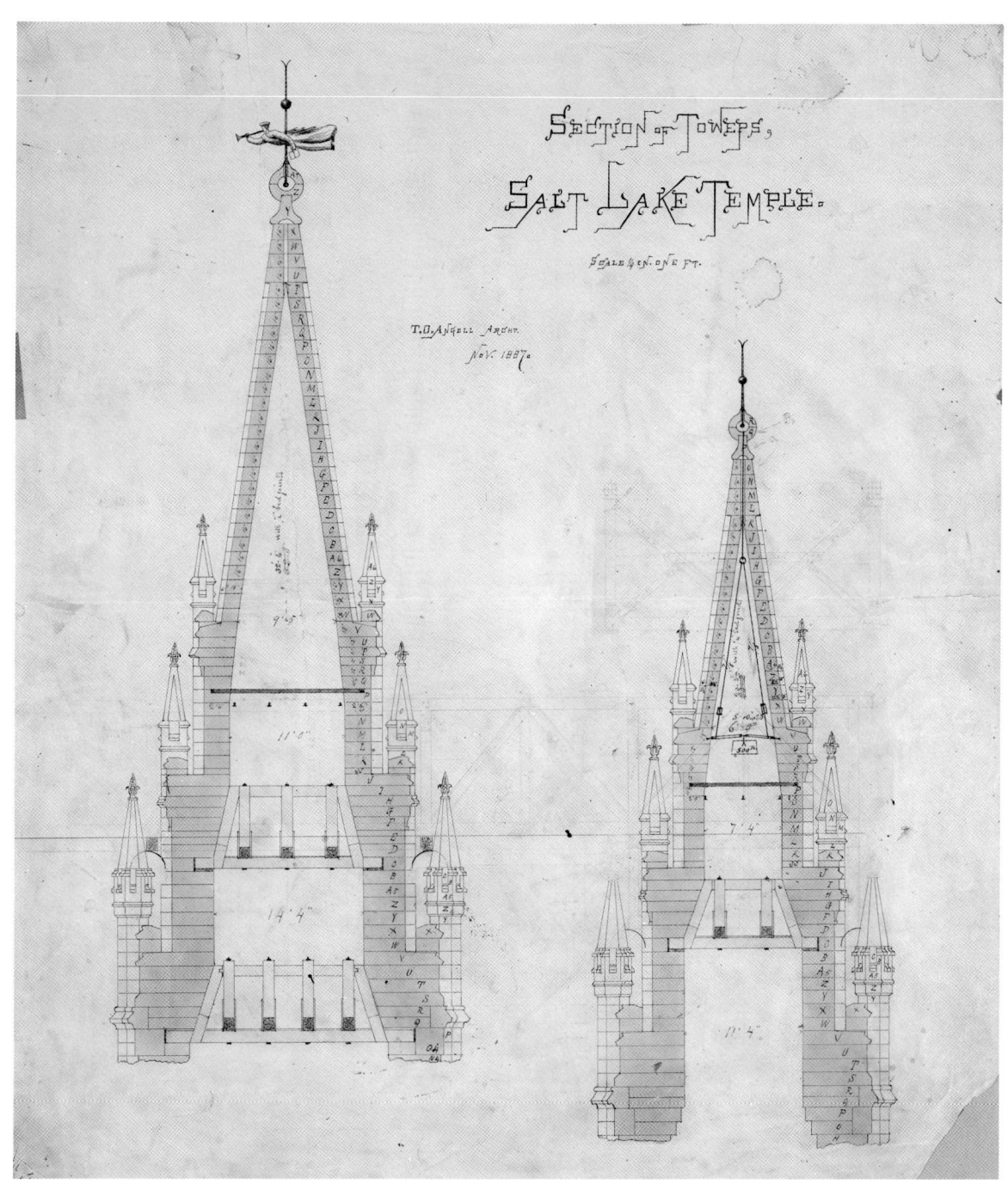

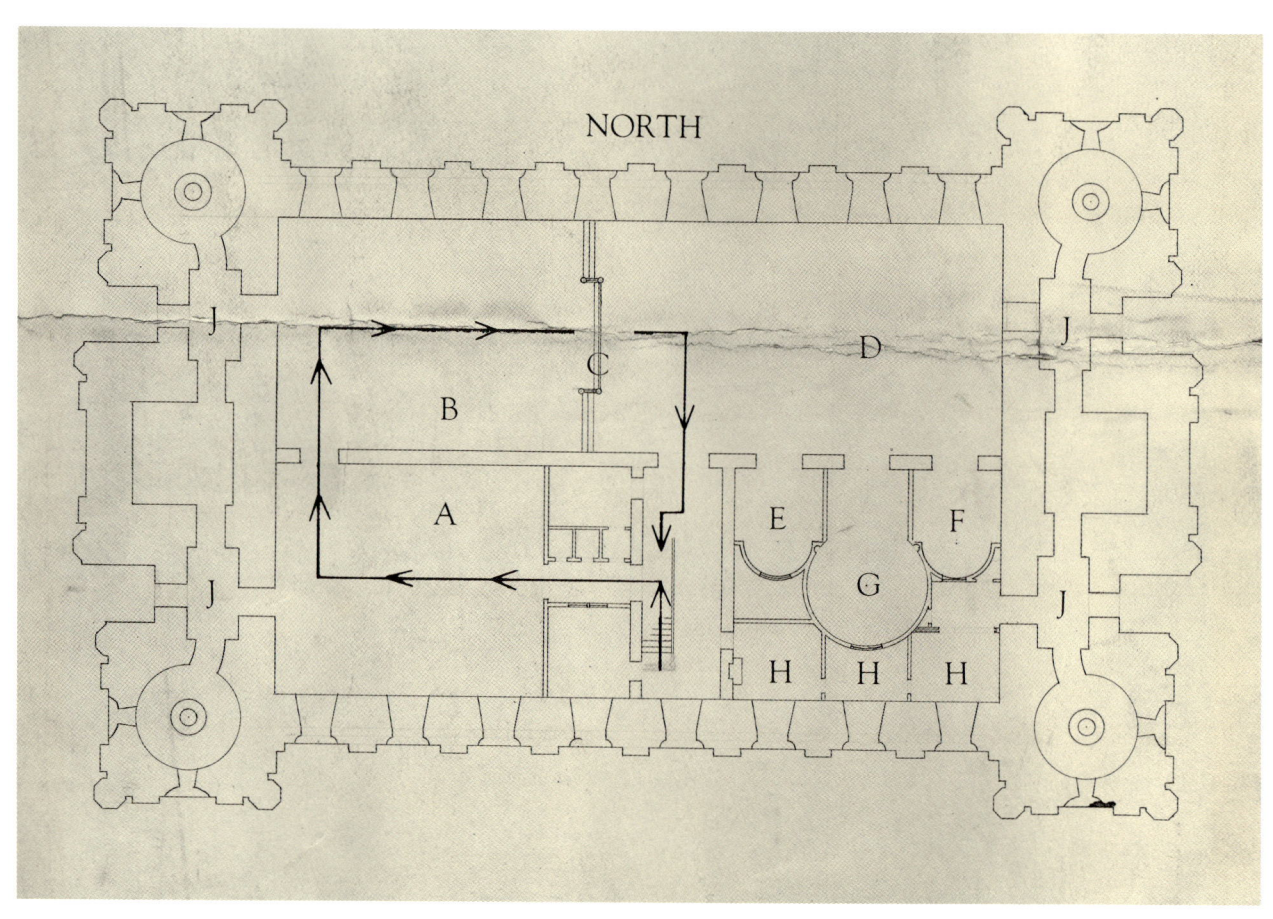

Second floor as completed in 1893 by Joseph Don Carlos Young. A) Telestial Room; B) Terrestrial Room; C) Veil; D) Celestial Room; E) East Sealing Room; F) West Sealing Room; G) Holy of Holies; H) ante-rooms; I) second-floor service corridor; and J) vestibules to the corner tower staircases.

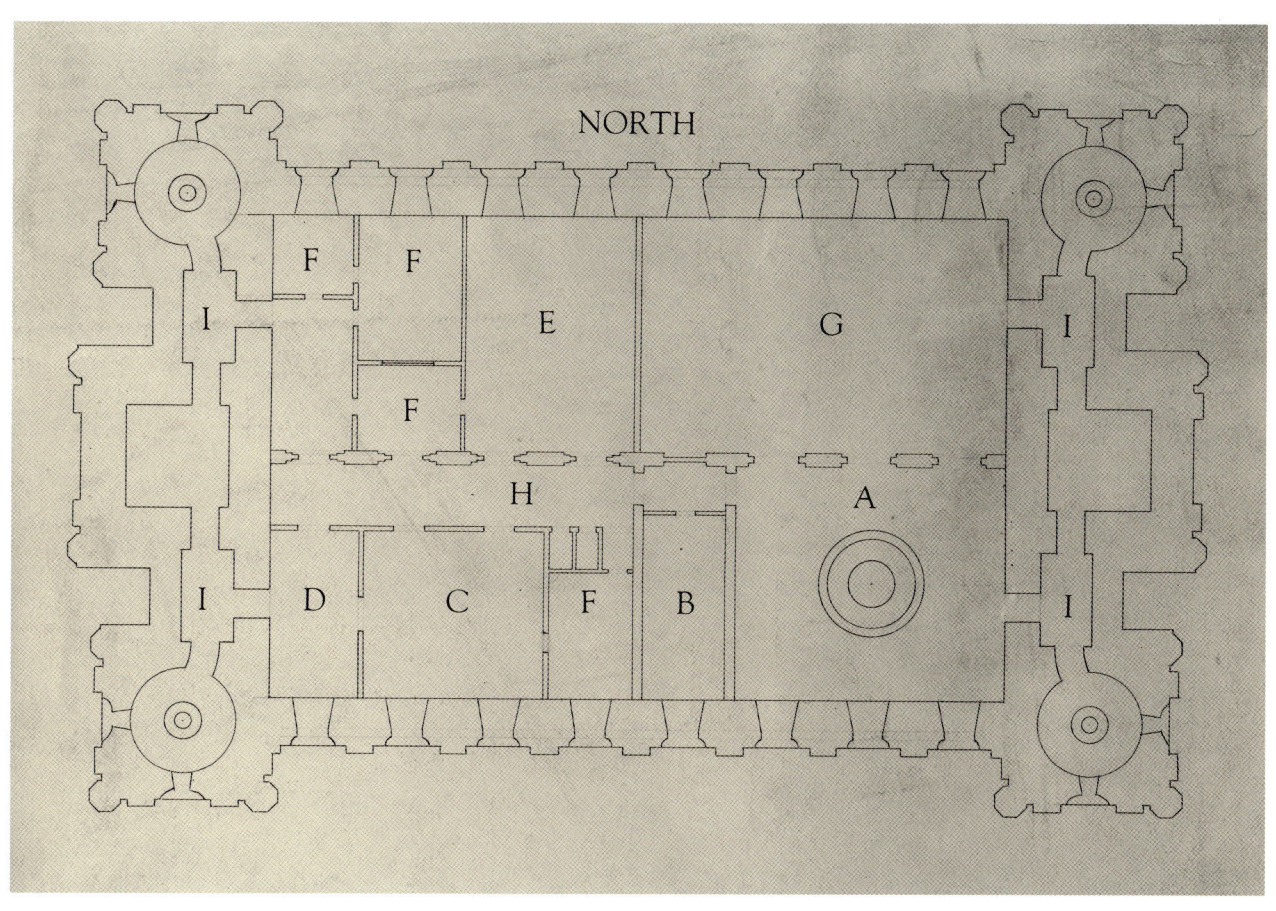

Third-floor council rooms as completed in 1893 by Joseph Don Carlos Young: A) Dome Room; B) Elders Room; C) Council Room of the Twelve Apostles; D) Council Room of the Seventy; E) Council Room of the First Presidency and the Twelve Apostles; F) ante-rooms; G) area occupied by the ceiling of the Celestial Room from the second floor; H) corridor; and I) vestibules to the corner tower staircases.

The 1893 photograph illustrates the copper finials that cap the four corner and west center spires. Each was ringed by eight incandescent bulbs that illuminated the upper structure of the Temple. The bulbs have since been removed, leaving the original finials.

John Taylor was the third president of the Church of Jesus Christ of Latter-day Saints and successor to Brigham Young. He approved the first major change in the original design of the Salt Lake Temple that affected the arrangement and spatial movement of the interior floors.

Wilford Woodruff, the fourth president of the Church of Jesus Christ of Latter-day Saints, dedicated the Salt Lake Temple on April 6, 1893. It was fitting that a close friend and trusted colleague to Brigham Young, who counselled with him on the Temple, should preside over its completion.

III

THE INTERIOR

THE INTERIOR

The change in the interior from a hall to a processional plan gave the Salt Lake Temple an added spatial dimension. The departure from the rigidity of the original single floor straight-line axial movement resulted in a greater sense of expectation in moving from one room to another as well as from floor to floor. The new flow pattern and compartmentalization gave each room its own character and reason for being.

Since 1893, the interior has undergone a number of cosmetic changes to update equipment and furnishings. The wood, except for the grand staircase, has been painted white to express an overall air of sanctity; and wall and ceiling murals replaced the plain surfaces of the Creation Room. These represent the major decorative alterations, while structurally the noticeable changes have been the passage area between the Terrestrial and Celestial Rooms and the attachment of a sealing annex to the north wall of the Temple. Otherwise the interior remains essentially unchanged.

The following photographic sequence illustrates the present interior appearance. Beginning at basement level, these pages proceed through the five functions of the Salt Lake Temple: the baptistry; the endowment rooms; the sealing rooms; the administrative floor; and the assembly hall. Continuing on the same sequential room order is a photographic display of the original interior of the Temple as it appeared in 1893. (Photographs taken by C. R. Savage in 1911.)

The Grand Staircase

Egressing from the Garden Room, the World or Telestial Room on the second floor is reached by the Grand Staircase at the south end of the access corridor. Because there is a rise in the level of the floor between the two lower lecture halls, the Garden Room exits onto the platform landing of the staircase.

The staircase is a fine example of late Victorian craftsmanship in rich cherry wood. From the heavy newel post, balusters, and handrail, the staircase ascends in a U-shape with a median landing. The staircase ends in a landing that is two steps lower than the level of the World Room to the west and six steps below the level of the Celestial Room to the north. The level of the second floor, where the remaining rooms associated with the endowment and sealing rituals are located, is determined from the outside by the first line of round-headed windows.

The Baptistry

Separating the baptistry from the two rooms to the east is a twelve-foot-wide corridor that extends the cross axial width of the Temple and acts as a narthex for both areas. It terminates at the south end with an elegant wooden grand staircase which leads to the above ground second floor. Its north end serves as the main entrance and exit point for the Temple. It is linked by passageways to the Temple Annex.

The baptistry occupies the west half of the basement. It consists of three compartments which are below ground to symbolize death and burial. The central room, being the largest, houses the six-by-ten-foot elliptical cast-iron baptismal font. It is large enough to hold 500 gallons of water to facilitate baptism by complete immersion (symbolic of death, burial and resurrection). In similitude of Solomon's "molten sea" and the twelve tribes of Israel, the font rests on the backs of twelve life-sized cast-iron oxen. The oxen are set three feet below the pavement of the main floor, possibly to accent the concept of burial and bring the font within perspective of those on the pavement level. The font is now reached by two staircases on either side of a platform that forms around the west end of the font. On the platform at the top of the stairs, there are places for the recorder and witnesses. The living proxies who act in behalf of the deceased enter the font by five short steps. There are attendant facilities to the west of the platform to care for those who have come from the font.

To the north and south of the baptistry are dressing rooms that open onto the font area through twelve arched double glazed doors.

The Garden Room

The Garden Room is furnished with rich continuous wall-through-ceiling oil murals that represent the "earth as it was before sin entered and brought with it a curse; it is the Garden of Eden in miniature." Cast in pervading greens, yellows, and subtle blues, the mural depicts a luxuriant landscape with birds, insects, and beasts living in harmony.

The Garden Room maintains the orientation and size of the previous lecture hall but now centers on a richly upholstered prayer altar on the south wall. The altar is raised on a three-step platform that is limited by flanking balustrades. On the south wall and to each side of the altar are two shallow service niches that are formed from the window recesses of the inner wall.

Telestial (World) Room

At the median landing of the Grand Staircase is a Tiffany stained glass window depicting the expulsion of Adam and Eve from the Garden of Eden. It symbolically reinforces the lecture of the Garden Room and prepares one for entrance into the Telestial Room, representing the world in which we live.

The Telestial Room forms the southwest quadrant of the second floor and rests on the ceiling trusses of the baptistry. On either side of the altar on the west wall are two round arched portals which enter into vestibule compartments. The larger portal to the south of the altar opens into the southeast corner vestibule and is on the level of the lecture hall. The north portal is considerably higher on the wall necessitating a steep staircase. It leads to the elevator vestibule of the west center tower and also interconnects with a similar staircase in the adjoining Terrestrial Room.

In contrast to the Garden Room, the Telestial Room is embellished by a continuous mural of the earth in a fallen rather than an exalted state.

Interior Tiffany stained glass round window over six feet in diameter dramatically portrays Adam and Eve being expelled from the Garden of Eden.

Telestial Room (continued from previous page)

Terrestrial Room

The classically appointed Terrestrial Room continues the clockwise movement of the previous areas with a west-east axial orientation. Entering at the southwest from the Telestial Room, it is symbolically elevated one step or level to stress a drastic change in the implied environment. The carnage and strife of the Telestial Room give way to a room completely devoid of such images. The intent was to illustrate the marked doctrinal and environmental differences between the rewards of these two kingdoms. The new indirect lighting system, crystal chandeliers, and mirrors enhance the effect of increased spirituality.

Behind the altar is a raised platform and the Veil. Both were later enlarged to accommodate the movement of a greater number of people between the Terrestrial and Celestial Rooms. The Veil is in similitude of one in the Tabernacle of Moses and the temple of Solomon. To pass through it into the Celestial Room is to symbolize one's passage and acceptance into the Kingdom of God or the highest degree of spiritual reward.

Celestial Room

The endowment ritual concludes upon entrance into the Celestial Room. The symbolic importance of the room is apparent from its increased size. The most obvious dimensional change is its thirty-four-foot-high ceiling. The spatial expansion was a deliberate effort to express visually a feeling of exaltation and a spiritual terminus. The concept of a terminus is suggested by the absence of an altar and the accustomed attached and oriented row seating. Instead, luxuriously appointed chairs and couches are placed in formal conversational arrangements. The furniture is set within an environment designed to imply the majesty that one would associate with the Kingdom of God. The complexity of gilded classical and baroque forms speaks of the then contemporary Ecole des Beaux Arts tradition in the manner of Richard Morris Hunt. The Celestial Room does not exhibit the restraint of the Terrestrial Room.

One of the few stained glass windows in the Salt Lake Temple not made by Tiffany. This window was designed and created locally.

THE ENDOWMENT RITUAL AND ASSOCIATED ROOMS

For one to receive his endowments, he must hold membership in the Church through baptism and confirmation. It is also necessary for men to be ordained to the Melchizedek priesthood. For the living, these prerequisite ordinances are performed outside the temple and on the basis of personal worthiness, whereas for the dead they are performed within the temple. After having received their own endowments, the living are expected to act as proxies in behalf of the deceased.

The sacred nature of the endowment and the associated temple ordinances are such that they cannot be discussed in any detail; but there is sufficient information available from reliable sources to convey the liturgical functions regarding the endowment. James E. Talmage best explains their significance:

> The temple endowment, as administered in modern temples, comprises instructions relating to the significance and sequence of past dispensations, and the importance of the present as the greatest and grandest era in human history. This course of instruction includes a recital of the most prominent events of the creative period [Creation Room], the condition of our first parents in the Garden of Eden, their disobedience and consequent expulsion from that blissful abode [Garden Room], their conditions in the lone and dreary world when doomed to live by labor and sweat, the plan of redemption by which the great transgression may be atoned, the period of the great apostacy, the restoration of the Gospel with all its ancient powers and privileges [Telestial Room], the absolute and indispensable condition of personal purity and devotion to the right in present life, and a strict compliance with Gospel requirements [Terrestrial Room].

The Creation Room

The presentation of the endowment lectures commences in the Creation Room in the northeast quadrant of the basement level. It is reached through a large round arched double glazed doorway from the axial corridor. The room is forty by forty-five feet with a north-to-south orientation. An arched doorway in the center of the south wall is the portal to the adjoining Garden Room. It was originally designed to seat two hundred and fifty people in folding chairs. After renovation, the seating capacity was increased to three hundred and one in more comfortable attached and cushioned folding chairs (similar changes, in seating capacity and furniture, transformed the Garden, Telestial and Terrestrial Rooms). The room as completed in 1893 was left unadorned but has since been decorated by an encompassing wall-and-ceiling mural depicting the stages of the earth's creation.

Above: *An original folding chair, prior to replacement by the cushioned chairs.*

SEALING ORDINANCES AND ROOMS

Associated with the endowment ceremony are the sealing ordinances performed for the living, specifically marriage for time and eternity and the sealing of children to parents who were not previously married in the Temple but civilly. The same ordinances are enacted for the deceased by living proxies in the belief that families can remain together as a distinct unit after death if they are sealed by the Holy Priesthood. Those who are to be sealed for the dead or themselves kneel about an altar and are sealed by an appointed officiator.

Along the south wall and two steps above the floor of the Celestial Room are three central doorways fitted with sliding doors. The east and west doors open into sealing rooms that form part of the southeast quadrant. The apse of the east room is centered by a small access door that opens into the south waiting room. The apse of the west room is dominated by a large stained glass window depicting the resurrected Angel Moroni delivering the gold plates to Joseph Smith. The rooms are similarly decorated and accented with a richly upholstered altar.

A third sealing room is located in the east center tower off the Celestial Room. It is reached by a quarter-turn staircase from the floor of the Celestial Room. A new two-story fourteen-room sealing annex for both the living and the dead was added to the north side of the Temple (1963-66). In sympathy with the design and materials of the Temple, it has been effectively mated to the height of the first level of windows. The annex is reached from within the Temple through a door formed from a window in the north wall of the Celestial Room. It has its own integrated staircase and elevator that gives access from the Annex complex.

The above Tiffany stained glass window depicts Joseph Smith receiving sacred plates from Angel Moroni. Right: The east Sealing Room, looking south from the Celestial Room.

THE DESIGN FOR ADMINISTRATION AND ASSEMBLY

The Salt Lake Temple was designed to serve two functions. Like all temples, it accommodated the needs of the temple ritual; but unlike the others, it was conceived as a place of council where the General Authorities could meet and decide on the doctrinal and administrative matters affecting the Church. Associated with the place of council is the place of assembly where selected people can gather and be taught by Church authorities the doctrines and policies affecting their lives.

The third floor comprises the area of the council chambers. It is recognized from the exterior by the first elevation of oval windows. As completed, less than half the area of the third floor is devoted to council rooms. The other area is occupied by the ceilings of the Celestial and Dome Rooms and an east-west axial corridor.

Tiffany stained glass window of the Temple, located on the administrative floor. The inscription to the left reads "Cornerstone laid April 6, 1853, by President Brigham Young, assisted by his counsellors, Heber C. Kimball, Willard Richards." To the right the inscription reads "Dedicated April 6, 1893, by President Wilford Woodruff, assisted by his counsellors George Q. Cannon, Joseph F. Smith."

The eight-foot-wide corridor begins at the Dome Room and runs seventy-five feet west to the west tower vestibule. On either side of the corridor are the council rooms which are rectangular with their long axes oriented north-south.

The eight-foot-wide corridor of the administrative floor.

A recent view of the Council Room of the First Presidency and the Twelve Apostles. From this chamber the law does "go forth" out from the "mountain of the Lord's House." (Isaiah 2:2, 3)

The Main Assembly Hall

The Assembly Hall occupies the entire area of the fourth floor between the two tower complexes. It is one hundred and twenty by eighty feet. The area is distinguished on the exterior by the two upper window courses. The main floor is at the level of the second course of round-headed windows. Its expansive wood floor terminates at the east and west ends with four-tiered officiating stands. They are for the respective priesthoods—Aaronic and Melchizedek. Their uppermost tier is canopied with an inscription denoting which priesthood. On the east is the Melchizedek or Higher priesthood and on the west, the Aaronic or Lesser priesthood. Melchizedek being the presiding priesthood of the Church—and in conformity with the arrangement of the towers—the east stand is physically higher than the one to the west.

The concept for the stands was derived from the pattern of those in the Kirtland and Nauvoo Temples. They are, however, open in design rather than closed box tiers. Though open, they are fronted by decorative balustrades and centered on a single large lectern flanked by two smaller book stands.

The original furniture of the main auditorium floor was designed to be reversible like that of Kirtland and Nauvoo. It could be changed to face the appropriate stand determined by which priesthood was officiating. The reversible benches were replaced by individual, lightly upholstered commercial folding chairs. They are unattached and can be easily set up or taken down.

The galleries, which are physically attached to the wall and located between the second course of round-headed and oval windows, are reached by four spiral staircases, located in the corners of the hall.

The Tower Staircases

The Main Assembly Hall and all other stories of the Temple are reached by four corner tower staircases. There are one hundred and seventy-seven granite steps to each staircase with the individual steps weighing over seventeen hundred pounds. They are attached to a center granite shaft of four feet in diameter creating a spiral movement. Its spiral design and monumental character is reminiscent of staircases found in medieval cathedrals and fortresses. There are two elevators in the west central tower whose shafts were part of the original plan. They were designed to augment the spiral staircases.

In addition to providing a holy place where Church leaders may meet, the interior program was specifically designed to facilitate the endowment and sealing ordinances. Temples are built in supplication of the presence of God that He may endow recipients or reveal from Heaven the eternal ordinances essential to the exaltation and eternal life of man.

The upper assembly hall was an architectural feature common to all nineteenth-century LDS Church temples, while infrequent in twentieth-century designs. The presence of the Holy of Holies and the administrative function of the third floor makes the Salt Lake Temple unique among temples and other ecclesiastical buildings of the Church.

The following pages are the sequential photographic display and order of rooms of the original interior of the Salt Lake Temple as it appeared in 1893. The photography is by C. R. Savage, circa 1911. The exceptional high quality and clarity in these photographs are the result of a special German screening technique, reproducing from the original glass plates which have been stored in the Church Archives for eighty years. This sequence is the first reproduction in print of these glass plates.

Left: The east portals of the Salt Lake Temple encase doors of oak with decorative brass hinges and grillwork. The doors are split finish—oak on the outside with oak-grain finished painted pine inside. This type of construction prevented warping and was very common for the period, oak not being an indigenous wood. Central to the theme are the cast brass beehives, symbol of industry. Entrance to the sanctuary is commonly through an underground tunnel connecting with the annex on the north side.

The baptismal font, supported by twelve axially arranged oxen similar to that of the Nauvoo and early Utah temples. Note the presence of protective railings and the east steps to the font.

Below: The Creation Room, looking south, before the addition of floor-to-ceiling murals. The portal leads to the Garden Room to the south.

Upper right: The Garden Room, looking northwest from the east balustrade of the altar. The portal door exits to the first landing of the grand staircase.

Lower right: The Garden Room, looking south from the portal entrance from the Creation Room. Note the original folding chairs.

The upper corridor looking north to the entrance portal to the Celestial Room and the entrance portal to the corridor of the Telestial or World Room.

The Telestial or World Room corridor looking east towards the grand staircase. Observe the original placement of the stained glass window of Adam and Eve's expulsion from the Garden of Eden.

Below: The Telestial or World Room, looking northwest towards the entrance portal of the Terrestrial Room to the right of the staircase.

Right: Stained glass depiction of Adam and Eve's expulsion from the Garden of Eden.

Below: The Terrestrial Room, looking southwest. Notice the more luxuriantly appointed chairs than those found in the previous rooms.

Right: The Terrestrial Room to the east towards the Veil.

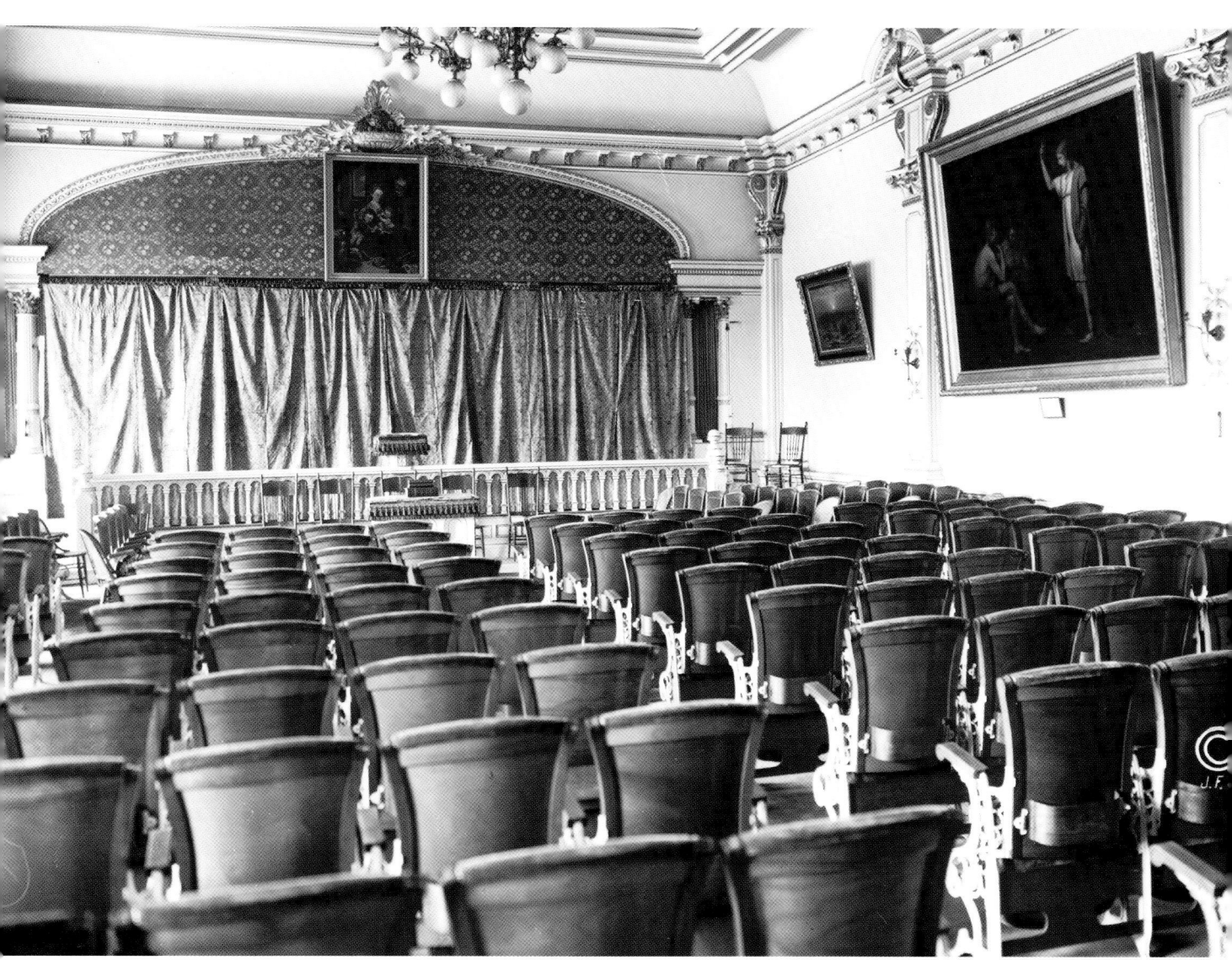

The Celestial Room, looking to the southeast toward the Sealing Rooms and the entrance to the Holy of Holies. The first door (only partially visible in photograph) accesses the upper corridor of the grand staircase; the second door, the west Sealing Room; the next door, the Holy of Holies. The far door accesses the east Sealing Room.

Left: The Celestial Room, looking west. Note the prominent position of mother and children sculpture above the veil.

Right: The west Sealing Room, looking south from the Celestial Room. The woodwork is painted lodgepole pine, an indigenous wood to the region. The original paints were locally manufactured and pigmented with dyes from the flowers of the hills and valleys.

The east Sealing Room, looking south from the Celestial Room.

Reception room, looking north, for guests and those waiting to be sealed. The open door portal gives a view through the east Sealing Room to the light from the north window of the Celestial Room.

The interior of the Holy of Holies towards the Tiffany stained glass depicting the First Vision.

Stained glass First Vision.

Below: The Council Room for the First Presidency and the Council of the Twelve Apostles. Again notice the change in furniture and the decorative character of the room.

Right: Elders' Prayer Room.

The Council Room of the Quorum of the Twelve Apostles, looking northwest toward twin double-door entrances to the administrative level corridor. The entrance on the left facilitated communication between the Quorum of the Twelve and the Presidents of the First Council of Seventy.

Below: The Main Assembly Hall has changed little since the dedication of the Temple in 1893.

Right: Like the Main Assembly Hall, corner tower staircases have changed little.

One of four corner tower granite spiral staircases.

IV
THE SYMBOLISM OF THE EXTERIOR

Oliver Cowdery, he received from the hands of Moses the "keys of the gathering of Israel from the four parts of the earth and the leading of the ten tribes from the land of the north." This doctrine of literal gathering required that there be a physical place to which people could gather. Missouri was designated as that place; but due to the Saints' expulsion from that state and later from the temporary site of Nauvoo, Salt Lake City became the alternate place of assemblage.

The Great Basin region was seen as the place of gathering. The Saints' removal to this area was no mistake. As early as 1842, Joseph Smith spoke of the Saints' withdrawal to the Rocky Mountains and persisted in this belief to his martyrdom. Brigham Young, on assuming the leadership of the Church upon Joseph Smith's death, continued in the thought of establishing his people in the protection of the mountains. Their direction came from a belief in Isaiah's prophecy of a literal gathering of the Lord's people to the "top of the mountains."

> And it shall come to pass in the last days, that the mountain of the Lord's house shall be established in the top of the mountains, and shall be exalted above the hills; and all nations shall flow unto it.
>
> And many people shall go and say, Come ye, and let us go up to the mountain of the Lord, to the house of the God of Jacob; and he will teach us of his ways, and we will walk in his paths; for out of Zion shall go forth the law, and the word of the Lord from Jerusalem. (Isaiah 2:2-3)

Central to Isaiah's prophecy was the "house of the God of Jacob." To LDS people, this refers to the Temple where one is taught the fullness of the doctrines of Christ and receives the ordinances necessary to dwell with God. On April 6, 1853, at the laying of the cornerstone, President Brigham Young said:

> Your endowment is to receive all those ordinances in the House of the Lord, which are necessary for you, after you have departed this life, to enable you to walk back to the presence of the Father, passing the angels who stand as sentinels, being enabled to give them the key words, the signs and tokens, pertaining to the Holy Priesthood, and gain eternal exaltation in spite of earth and hell.

It is significant that the Salt Lake Temple was designed from the outset to function solely in the capacity of sacred space; because it is here where God could dwell within walls dedicated for that purpose. The combined presence of the Temple and the established headquarters of the Church (with a prophet at its head who professes continued communication with God) appear to satisfy Isaiah's prophecy. In reference to Isaiah, the Temple has become more than the physical symbol of the Church. It has become the "spiritual ensign to the world."

The siting of the Temple on the east-west axis of Temple Square places it at right angles to the north-south axial movement of Temple Square. Even when seen at its most picturesque angle, the Temple exerts no compelling outreach to bring one in line with its entrance nor any visual suggestion to approach the structure. The sanctuary walls project the feeling of enclosure but do not function to draw one in. A broader perspective of Temple Square and the Salt Lake Temple, however, reveals a more comprehensive siting and symbolic program that reaches beyond the ten-acre sanctuary. It will appear that Brigham Young selected the Temple site with the prophecy of Isaiah in mind.

The geographical location of Salt Lake City fulfills Isaiah's requirements for "mountain" in two interpretations. The first is literal and plural and the second figurative and singular. The literal can be represented by the adjoining Wasatch and Oquirrh Mountain ranges that reach out to draw in those who have sought the security of the Salt Lake Valley with its temple. Whether in fulfillment of prophecy or by coincidence, the assemblage of the natural with the man-made has created an appropriate place for gathering as spoken of by Isaiah.

Once vectored to the Temple and within the protective walls of Temple Square, the individual is removed from the common environment of the outside world to one of quiet seclusion. Within this sacred enclosure, Brigham Young saw the Temple as the place from where the "law shall go forth" and as the compendium of LDS belief. He made provisions in the original plans for the Temple to incorporate numerous symbols that functioned with medieval complexity to speak of the order of God, Christ, the restoration of His gospel, man's relationship to Him and the proclamation to the world of His reality. Brigham Young's theological statement was encompassing when compared to Joseph Smith's embryo program of moon-, sun-, and star-stones on the Nauvoo Temple. Today the significance of the symbols is lost in a period when they are of little supposed value. In order to approach their meaning, one must have an understanding of LDS doctrine, practice, and scripture, along with the information given by Truman O. Angell, Sr., and a study of the Temple plans.

In 1878, a plan of the Temple's exterior walls was purposely drafted to plot the exact location of each of the fifty moon-stones according to lunar phase, month and year. This was determined by observations made that year in anticipation of the next season's building program when the moon-stones were to be laid. The individual most capable of such an observation was Orson Pratt (1811-1881). He was a professor of astronomy at the University of Nauvoo and later the University of Deseret (now the University of Utah) in Salt Lake City. Not only was he competent in astronomy but also in other areas, including Hebrew. On November 11, 1850, he received international recognition in advanced mathematics for his theory of the law governing planetary rotation. The Saints knew of his brilliance in astronomy through a series of twelve open lectures on that subject during the winter and spring of 1851-1852. He held similar lectures in the early part of 1871. His later discourses attracted such large crowds that they were held in the Tabernacle. A member of the Council of the Twelve Apostles, he devoted most of his time to the Church. When not on one of his seven missions to England and Europe and at least another eleven in the United States, he spent his time attending to his studies. In 1869, an astronomical observatory of wood and adobe was constructed specifically for him on the southeast corner of the Temple Block. It fittingly faced the southeast corner of the Temple. It was equipped with the instruments he brought from Nauvoo and those supplied by the United States Government in order that he could make more accurate observations and measurements.

To date, there are no recorded accounts of shared knowledge between Brigham Young and Orson Pratt over the symbolism of the Temple, even though they often discussed doctrinal matters. Brigham Young was, however, aware of his investigations and their eternal implications. It may be significant that before the first Temple plans appeared in 1853, Orson Pratt had just completed his lecture series, and a brief text of their contents was published in the *Deseret News* a year later when the Temple plans were still in preparation. In 1874, Truman O. Angell, Sr., spoke of the symbols and defined some of their meanings. This came on the heels of Orson Pratt's 1871 lectures which were printed in full in the *Deseret News* of that year. His appointment as Church Historian in 1874 brought him even closer to the office and affairs of the Church.

There was never a time in the history of the Church when its members were so well informed on the matters of astronomy. At the same time, there was never a people better prepared to understand and appreciate the iconographic programs on the Temple than they. As plotted in 1878, the lunar sequence begins on the north wall with the fifth buttress from the northwest corner tower (designated as buttress two on the plan) and continues in a clockwise movement around the fifty buttresses of the Temple. The sequence logically ends with the point of starting, but more specifically, between the new and first quarter moons of buttresses four and five from the northwest corner tower. The specific reason for fifty moon-stones was to create a sequential break to establish the beginning point of the lunar cycle.

The same clockwise progression is seen in the correct order in which temples are to be laid out. As explained by Joseph Smith:

> If the strict order of the Priesthood were carried out in the building of Temples, the stones would be laid at the southeast corner by the First Presidency of the Church. The southwest corner should be laid next. The third, or northwest corner next; and the fourth, or northeast corner last. The First Presidency should lay the southeast cornerstone and dictate who are the proper persons to lay the other cornerstones.

> If a Temple is built at a distance, and the First Presidency are not present, then the Quorum of the Twelve Apostles are the persons to dictate the order for that Temple; and in the absence of the Twelve Apostles, then the Presidency of the Stake will lay the southeast cornerstone; the Melchizedek Priesthood laying the cornerstones on the east side of the Temple, and the Lesser Priesthood those on the west side.

On April 6, 1853, Brigham Young had the Salt Lake Temple laid out in this prescribed order.

The restoration of the Gospel is symbolized by the angel Moroni set atop the spire of the center tower of the east facade. He is depicted as the herald spoken of by John the Revelator.

> And I saw another angel fly in the midst of heaven, having the everlasting gospel to preach unto them that dwell on the earth, and to every nation, and kindred, and tongue, and people,
>
> Saying with a loud voice, Fear God, and give glory to him; for the hour of his judgment is come: and worship him that made heaven, and earth, and the sea, and the fountains of waters. (Revelations 14:6-7)

According to LDS belief, the announcement of the impending restoration of the gospel of Christ, as symbolized by the angel Moroni atop the east center spire, was soon followed by the restoration of the priesthood. The six-tower/spire configuration is emblematic of this authority on earth and therefore presides in architectural complexity over the Temple. This priesthood is administered by authorities who direct the Church through the established doctrine of divine and continued revelation. The east tower grouping is purposely six feet higher (210) than those of the west to represent the higher or Melchizedek Priesthood which is the authority to preside over the spiritual affairs of the Church. Its three towers represent the presiding authorities—namely, the President of the Church and his two counselors. They are also symbolic of the local stake leadership of Stake President and his two counselors. The twelve finial spires atop the corner buttresses of each tower represent the Twelve Apostles and their local jurisdictional equivalents. The west towers, being lower (204) in elevation, represent the lesser or Aaronic Priesthood. Its three towers are emblematic of the Presiding Bishop and his two counselors and their local equivalents. Truman O. Angell, Sr., mentioned that the finial spires of the east and west tower groupings represent the Twelve Apostles. His interpretation came from one of Brigham Young's visits to his office during the preliminary design phase of the Salt Lake Temple. Years later, as reported in the *Deseret News,* William Ward, who was in attendance, referred to the President's remarks:

> There will be three towers on the east, representing the President and his two counselors; also three towers on the west representing the Presiding Bishop and his two

counselors; the towers on the east, the Melchizedek Priesthood, those on the west the Aaronic Priesthood. The centre towers will be higher than those on the sides, and the west towers a little lower than those on the east end.

Subsequent to the restoration of the priesthood authority and the founding of the Church was the commission by the Savior to take the gospel to all the inhabitants of the earth. As observed from the original Temple plans, there were to be cloud-stones with descending rays of light placed just below the caps of the inside buttresses of the four corner towers. They represented the gospel being taken to the four corners of the earth "to every nation, and kindred, and tongue, and people." They were "emblematic of the gospel light piercing through the clouds dispelling the clouds of superstition and error which had engulfed the world." It is significant that they were placed on the priesthood towers because missionary work is a function of the priesthood and the four corner towers were statements of the four corners of the earth with the center towers being a statement of the priesthood authority.

The missionary concept is in harmony with the iconography of the constellation Ursa Major (Big Dipper) on the center tower of the west facade. It is the symbol of the priesthood or those ordained of the Lord sent to administer "to the Lost" who "may find their way by the aid of the priesthood." These inhabitants of the earth are symbolized by the earth-stones which are the reciprocal emblem to the cloud-stones with Ursa Major as the intercessor symbol.

The dedicatory inscription, set below the cloud-stones, symbolizes the reality of the establishment of His kingdom on earth with the Temple as His personal sanctuary where heaven and earth are joined in a perfect order. It is also the place (as are any of the temples) where the inhabitants of Zion or those pure in heart can gather and be taught of light and truth.

> ...Literally the house of the Lord... a house where he and his Spirit may dwell, to which he may come or send his messengers, to confer priesthood and keys and to give revelation to his people.

Beneath the previous symbols and in descending order from heavenly to earthly is the so-called All-Seeing Eye. It is set in the arch of the second major window of both facades. This ancient motif has multiple applications, but, in reference to LDS doctrine, its translation is found in the books of Psalms and Proverbs (Psalms 33:18; Proverbs 15:3). The first is consistent with the concept of divine protection afforded those who seek to make God their friend. The second concerns the omnipresent nature of God and his ability to discern the good and evil deeds of man.

The inscription "I AM ALPHA AND OMEGA" on the keystone of the first major windows reaffirms Christ's eternal existence on which His people can lay their faith and be strengthened in their knowledge of His divinity. Set in the window arch, below the inscription, is the Clasped-Hand motif. It, like the All-Seeing Eye, is ancient in origin and has multiple applications. To Latter-day Saints, it represents the hand of fellowship within the eternal context of the gospel—man's relationship to man within the gospel of Christ.

The earth-stones terminate the descending order of sun- and moon-stones. As mentioned by Truman O. Angell, Sr., they were to be seen collectively as the dwelling place for man "where the gospel is to fill the world." This might seem a most naive conclusion to make at this juncture; but, it must be explained that LDS people believe the earth, in its present state of progression, is the lowest of God's creations. It also symbolizes the lowest of God's kingdoms of rewards. Its placement in the iconographic scheme is both appropriate and fitting to the position of mortal man who now must look heavenward.

Man, as a mortal, is now placed in a position of having to make a decision. The iconographic program to this point has taught him the reality of Christ and His mission of redemption and of the restoration of His church and priesthood in this present day. It is then his responsibility to act in order to determine which kingdom he will inherit. On fifty flat buttresses of the Temple is expressed in symbols the potential of man's reward in the life after death. The assembled earth-stones, moon-stones, and sun-stones are to be read vertically to represent the varying kingdoms of worthiness or reward. The earth or, in LDS vocabulary, the telestial kingdom, is the lowest, the moon or terrestrial kingdom is the middle and the sun or celestial is the highest kingdom. What might appear to be a discrepancy in this interpretation is not. Even though the glory of the telestial kingdom in LDS theology is likened unto the brightness of the stars, the earth can be given that designation also. The reality of the earth being the telestial kingdom is based on the LDS belief that the earth must pass through a series of stages in order to be exalted. With the fall of Adam, the earth fell to assume a fallen or telestial state. At the Lord's second coming, the earth will be cleansed to usher in the millennial era and begin a terrestrial state. The millennium will close with a "short period" in which Satan will be loosed; after which, the earth will die only to be resurrected and receive its celestial glory. It then becomes a fit abode for those who once lived on the earth and have earned the celestial order. This explains why the star-stones can be placed even above the sun-stones to represent the heavens; while at the same time, the earth can be designated as the telestial kingdom. The ultimate truth of this interpretation lies with the liturgy of the temples. Doctrinally, the vertical reading of the earth-stones, moon-stones, and sun-stones translate into the telestial, terrestrial, and celestial kingdoms of reward and the stages of the earth's progression. These emblematic stones have now taken on a double meaning. The iconographic scheme has now gone full cycle to establish a prescribed order.

When taken as a whole, the Temple, its geographic location, and its iconographic program can be seen as an overall established order concentric with the order of heaven. Integral to this order is the relationship between God and man. The intended program of the building is to aid man in his quest to gain entrance back into the presence of God from whence he came. The Temple is literally a compendium of LDS belief.

"And it shall come to pass in the last days, that the mountain of the Lord's house shall be established in the top of the mountains, and shall be exalted above the hills; and all nations shall flow unto it.

And many people shall go and say, Come ye, and let us go up to the mountain of the Lord, to the house of the God of Jacob; and he will teach us of his ways, and we will walk in his paths; for out of Zion shall go forth the law, and the word of the Lord from Jerusalem." (Isaiah 2:2-3)

The original 1855 drawing of the east facade by William Ward, Jr.

A general view of the east facade. Note the descending order of symbolic stones: beginning at the top of both end towers are Saturn-stones, star-stones, sun-stones, moon-stones, and earth-stones. From top to bottom on the center tower are the angel Moroni, cloud-stones, the dedicatory inscription, the All-Seeing Eye motif, the Alpha-Omega inscription, the clasped-hand motif, and earth-stones.

Angel Moroni atop the spire cap of the east center tower.

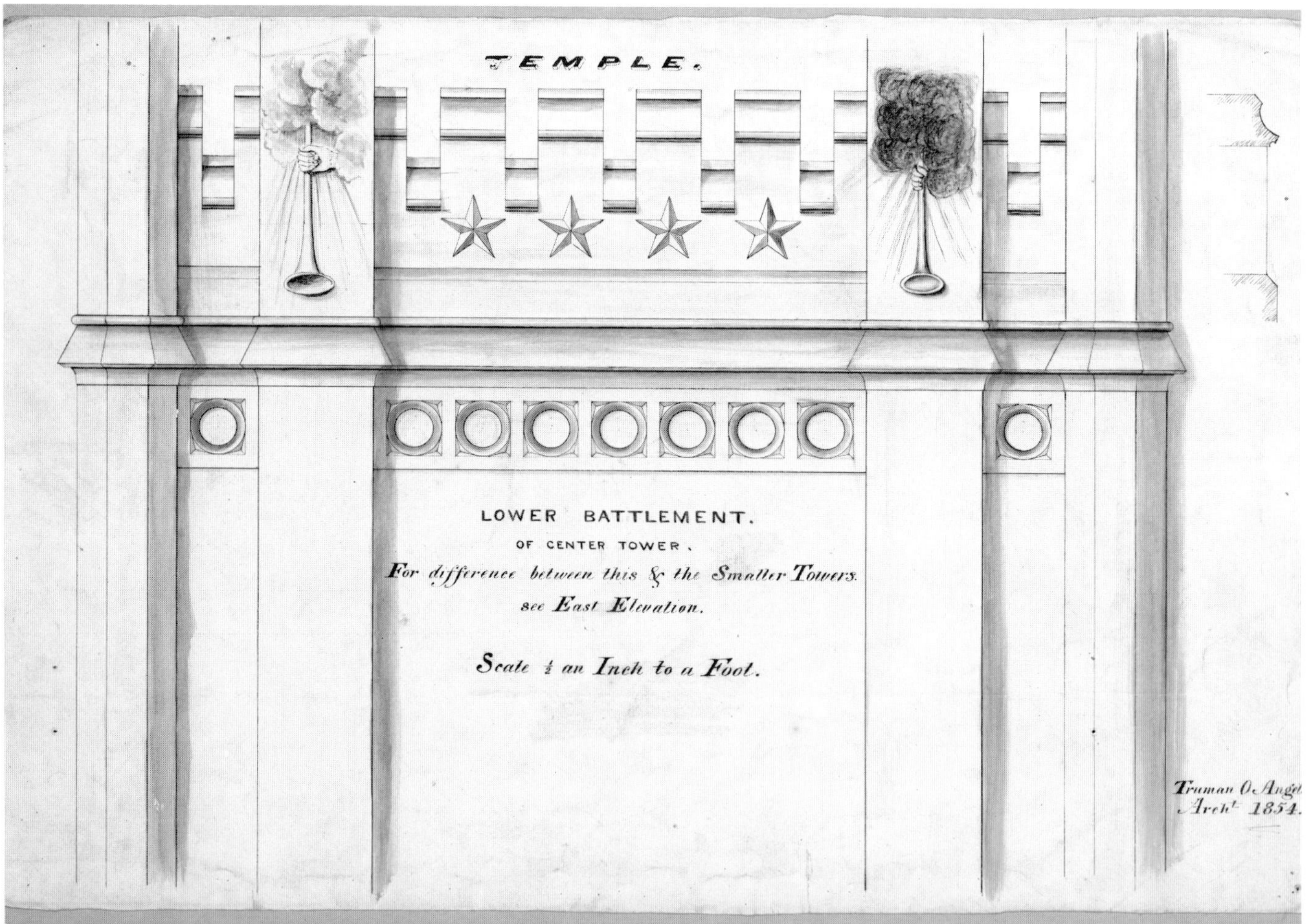

TEMPLE.

LOWER BATTLEMENT.
OF CENTER TOWER.
For difference between this & the Smaller Towers
see East Elevation.

Scale ¼ an Inch to a Foot.

Truman O. Angell
Archt. 1854.

Left: Close-up detail of east center tower showing cloud-stones and star-stones. Lower left: Note the original sketch by Truman O. Angell depicting the above. Right: The dedicatory inscription on the east center tower set below the cloud-stones. Below: Truman O. Angell's original architectural drawings, ca. 1855, of the dedicatory inscription on the east center tower, and the Alpha and Omega inscription with clasped-hand motif.

A detail of the All-Seeing Eye motif below the dedicatory inscription on the east center tower.

A detail of the Alpha-Omega inscription and the clasped-hand motif on the east center tower.

The original 1854 drawing of the south elevation by Truman O. Angell.

The south elevation of the Salt Lake Temple as it appeared at the turn of the century.

The intricate detail in Truman O. Angell's architectural drawing of the original exterior program of the south and east elevations is attributed to the type of building material that Brigham Young expected to use. He proposed that it be constructed with an inner core of adobe with a protective exterior veneer of freestone. The fine grain freestone was capable of taking such detail; but Wilford Woodruff persuaded Young to use granite, which resulted in the loss of intricate detail.

The above, showing the original drawing of the earth-stones from the plinths for the wall buttresses, differs from the actual photo below. The change in materials from freestone to granite eliminated the detail suggested in the original drawing.

A view of the present south elevation displaying the order of the symbolic stones. Below: The cycle of the lunar month—new, first quarter, full, and last quarter. Upper right: A detail of sun-stones. Lower right: A detail of the first quarter and new moon.

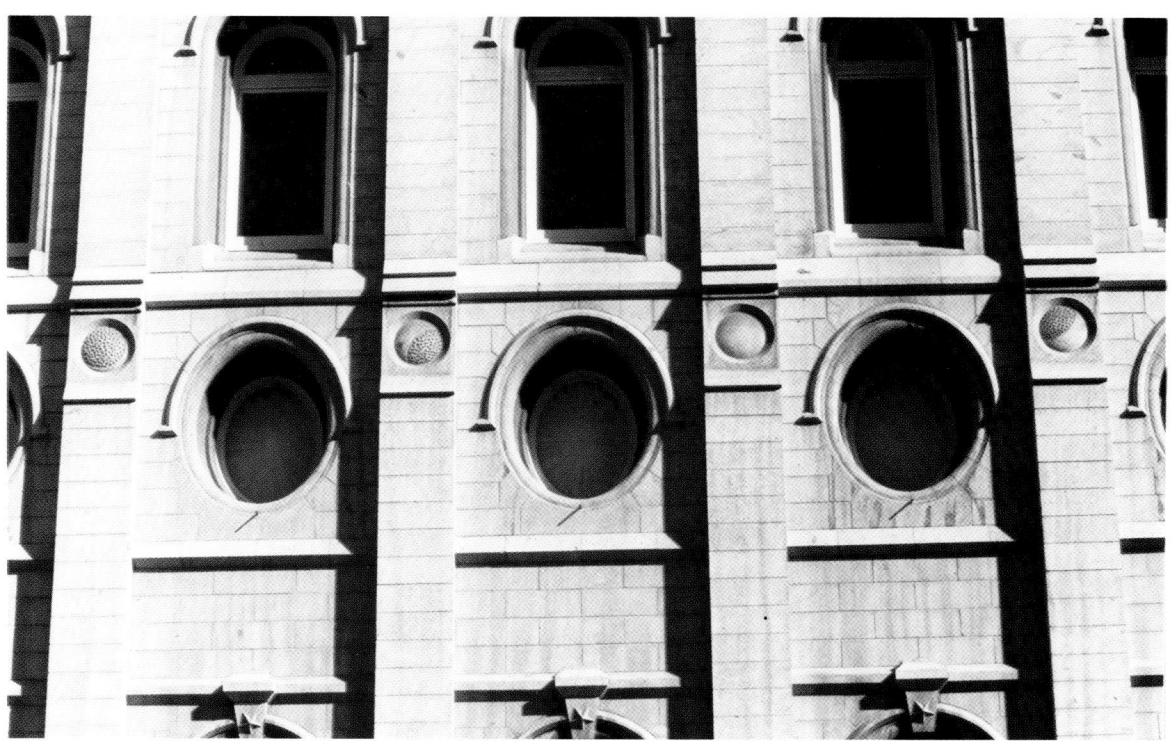

The sculptural niches on either side of the east and west central towers go unnoticed by the casual observer. Yet the eastern niches were designed, and housed at one time bronze figures of Joseph Smith and his brother Hyrum. The historical representations were removed from the niches and placed on plinths on the south lawn.

Hyrum Smith sustained his brother Joseph in all their activities. In 1844, following the lead of his brother, whom he believed to be a prophet of God, Hyrum surrendered with Joseph to the Illinois State Militia under command of the governor, who personally guaranteed their safety. Once the Smiths were in custody, the militia was released from command, reorganized themselves, and killed the brothers. Joseph had previously said that if he were taken into custody he would be murdered. However, he consented to surrender when some of the Church members expressed fear for their own safety. Hyrum was forty-four years old and Joseph was thirty-eight on June 27, 1844. As a result of that day's events, the mantle of leadership would fall upon Brigham Young.

Above: The multi-staged tower/spires of the Salt Lake Temple. Right: The constellation Ursa Major (Big Dipper) on the upper reaches of the west center tower.

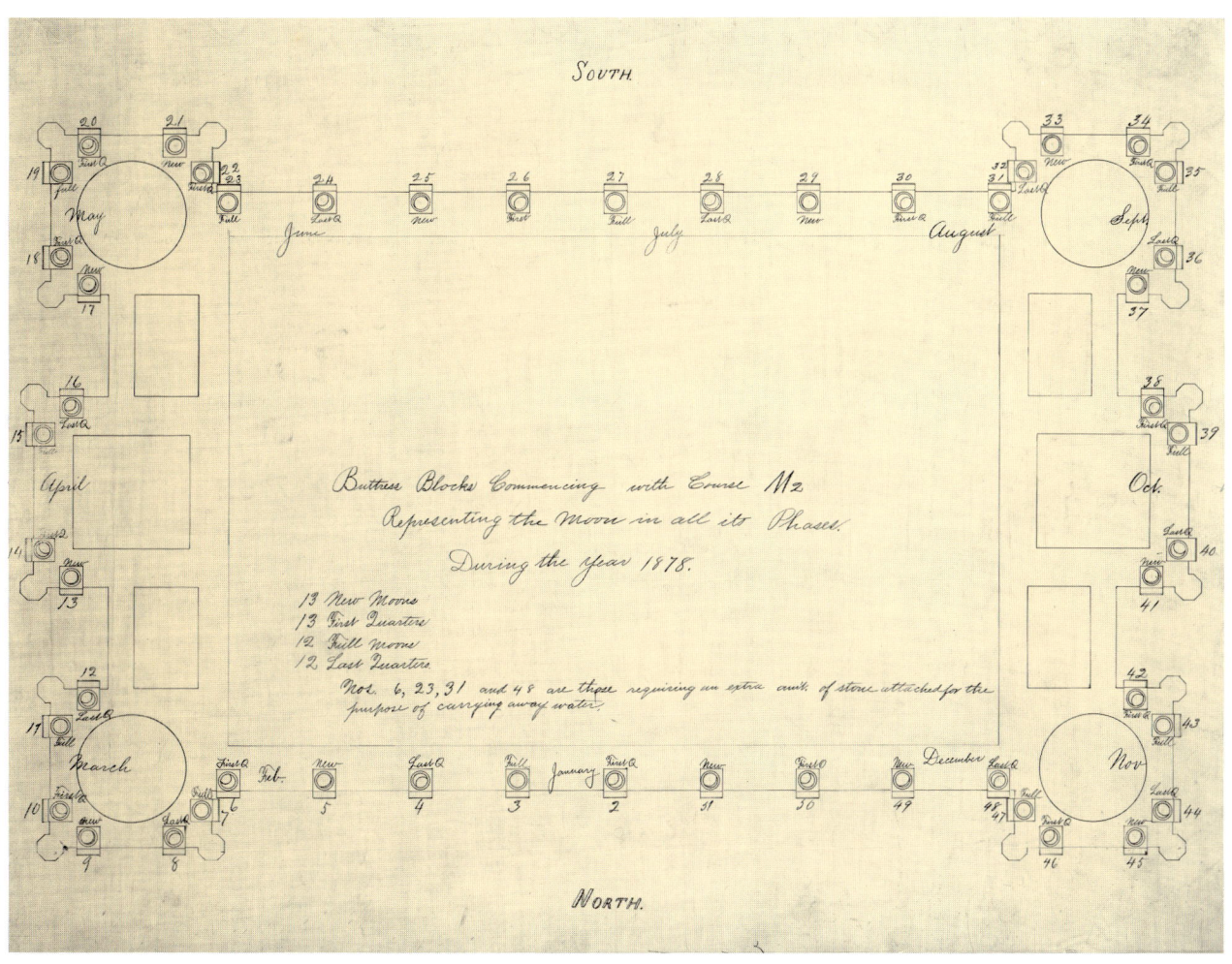

Orson Pratt's involvement in the symbolic program for the Salt Lake Temple is evident from an 1878 plan used to plot that year's lunar cycle in preparation for the laying of the fifty moon-stones.

Brigham Young's fascination with symbolism prompted him to build an observatory ornamented with a beehive atop his Beehive House. The beehive is a symbol of industry. It decorated the Temple and many of Brigham Young's designs. In the Book of Mormon the term "Deseret" meant honeybee. Hence, Brigham Young called the new territory the Territory of Deseret before statehood.

The Salt Lake Temple as it appeared in the 1890s, with Orson Pratt's observatory in the foreground.

Orson Pratt, considered by his contemporaries to be one of the world's leading mathematicians and astronomers, held well-attended lectures on astronomy in the Tabernacle for the Church membership. His lectures and their subsequent publication in the Church-owned newspaper gave the saints a knowledge of the order of our solar system and the universe, particularly as it pertained to the order of God's creations. So important were his studies that an adobe and wood astronomical observatory was constructed for him on the southeast corner of the Temple Block. It was from his observatory that his lunar observations for the Temple's moon-stones were made in 1878.

Exterior and interior of Pratt's observatory, near the turn of the century.

V
TEMPLE SQUARE

TEMPLE SQUARE

On Wednesday, July 28, 1847, just four days after the Saints' arrival in the valley of the Great Salt Lake, Brigham Young selected the site for the new temple. He originally intended the Temple Block to be forty acres but reduced it to ten, making a uniform city plat. The block was then divided equally, following the east-west, north-south orientation of the city.

During his lifetime, President Young envisioned the construction of several permanent buildings—the Salt Lake Temple, the Tabernacle, a bell tower, and the Assembly Hall. The Temple was sited in the center of the east end, the Tabernacle in the west end. At the point of convergence between the two buildings, he proposed the erection of a tower, most likely to house the bell that was brought from Nauvoo to call the Saints to camp meetings. Of the three buildings, the bell tower was never constructed.

Though he proposed only three permanent structures, a number of temporary buildings were erected during Young's tenure. The 1847 Bowery, constructed on the southwest corner of the block, was the first of these. Built by members of the Mormon Battalion in one day, it was constructed of conveniently acquired wooden posts, canopied by brush and willows on a simple lintel roof system. Like frontier boweries, it was designed specifically to shade congregations with the sides left open for ventilation. It was replaced the following year by a larger bowery, 160 feet long, in anticipation of more Saints. For the same reason the second bowery was replaced in 1851 by a more permanent structure.

The Old Tabernacle, completed in 1852, was a thick-walled adobe building topped by a medium pitched roof. It was unique because of its near full-width hemispherical apse at the north end. With a seating capacity of 2,500, the interior was not encumbered by posts, which accounts for the pitch of the roof and the arched ceiling. A multi-entrance building, it was designed as an all-weather structure with chimneys set near its four corners.

Because of the small capacity of the Old Tabernacle, a third bowery was built to the north to accommodate the ever-increasing numbers of Saints entering the Salt Lake Valley. President Young proposed its construction on July 24, 1854. It was intended to seat some 12,000 people, but actually accommodated only 8,000. On April 6, 1863, Heber C. Kimball proposed that it be razed to make way for the new Tabernacle to be built the next year.

Structurally the most innovative building on Temple Square, the second Tabernacle is an elliptical domed masterpiece of nineteenth-century engineering. Its dome, designed by Henry Grow, has an Ithiel Town lattice truss system and spans an area of 250 by 150 feet. The ceiling is 65 feet from the lowest point of the slope of the floor and 75 feet to the top of the roof. The dome is supported by 44 massive sandstone piers with 16 double-door entrances set among them for easy access to the building. Grow determined that the double doors could facilitate the egress of 13,000 people in five minutes (though no more than 8,000 could be seated).

On learning of the building's poor acoustics at its completion in 1867, Brigham Young asked that the problem be corrected. Truman O. Angell, Sr., designed and supervised the addition of a 30-foot-wide gallery in 1870. It is supported on a double row of wooden columns that are painted to appear as marble. It is attached to the back wall at 12- to 15-foot intervals, leaving a 2½-foot space between the gallery and the wall. The detached non-continuous gallery alleviated the problem of annoying echoes.

The focus of the interior is on the large rostrum and the 375-seat choir area that is continuous with the height of the gallery. Set above the choir seats is the large pipe organ of 11,000 pipes; the largest pipe, including its wooden structure, is 48 feet high. The Tabernacle became the first permanent building to be completed on the Temple Block.

In 1877 the Old Tabernacle was determined to be inadequate and was razed to make way for a new permanent structure on the same site. Stone for the new Assembly Hall, designed by Obed Taylor, came from discarded granite blocks from the Temple. They were neither cut nor dressed as those for the Temple, which accounts for the visible texture and broad masonry joints. The Hall's picturesque Victorian Gothic style, in sympathy with the style of the Temple, is enhanced by its rustic exterior finish.

The Assembly Hall's Gothic exterior and pseudo-cruciform plan is belied by a non-vaulted classically appointed interior. What could be mistaken from the outside for small transept arms are little more than shallow entrance recesses for the main floor and stairwells for the gallery. Except for the sloping decorative ceiling, its interior is similar to that of the Tabernacle. Its floor slopes to meet the rostrum at the west while a non-continuous gallery, supported by a single row of columns, form around three sides of the interior to terminate with the choir seats. Continuous in height to the gallery, the choir area above the rostrum is overshadowed by a large pipe organ whose pipes are set in a wood superstructure with the larger pipes exposed. When dedicated in 1882, it became the second permanent building to be completed on Temple Square. The building was rededicated following extensive renovation and the installation of a new organ in 1983.

The remaining buildings completed on the Temple Block through 1893 were those associated with the functions of the Temple. The first such building was the Salt Lake Endowment House. Acknowledging the length of time it would take to complete the Salt Lake Temple, and sensing the urgency for his people to receive their endowments and sealings, President Young called for the construction of a temporary structure to administer these ordinances. The northwest corner of the Temple Block was selected as the site for the new building. The simple rectangular two-story adobe structure was dedicated on May 5, 1855, by Heber C. Kimball. In the spring of 1889, after 34 years of continuous use, it was demolished. Its destruction came after the dedication of the St. George, Logan, and Manti Temples and four years prior to the opening of the Salt Lake Temple.

Designed by Joseph Don Carlos Young, the Old Annex was begun in 1892 and dedicated on April 6, 1893. It was the main entrance to the Temple by an underground access tunnel. The exterior was obviously inspired by Byzantine and possibly Moorish sources. Built of oolitic fine-grained limestone from the Manti quarries, it was sited north of the Temple. It was razed in 1962 to make way for a more adequate and architecturally compatible building.

The New Annex was completed in 1966 in a style reminiscent of fifteenth-century King's College Chapel at Cambridge, England. It was the last building associated with the function of the Temple. The remaining structures on Temple Square are for visitors.

The fifteen-foot adobe and sandstone wall that encloses the Temple Block is of greater significance to the creation of a religious sanctuary than any of the attendant buildings. The wall was started in 1852 as a make-work project to assist the newly arrived Saints and those making their way to the California gold fields. After a time, its construction was considered necessary to protect the growing amount of machinery that was collecting on the Temple Block. But of more importance, it kept the spirit of the Saints alive in preparation for the beginning of the Temple. Years later, the adobe bricks were plastered to protect them from exposure. Virtually all of the original wall has been replaced over the years.

What began as a make-work project turned into the one structure that isolated the Temple and its attendant buildings from secular metropolitan encroachment. The controlled space with the carefully manicured trees, grass, shrubs, and flower beds is responsible for an atmosphere of ordered reverence. This is in contrast to the congestion of the city outside the walls. Entering from the south, one notices that the Temple is set apart from the other buildings by its placement on a landscape terrace. Physically, the terrace was intended to correct the southwest slope of the ground, but it also established the hierarchical importance of the Temple over its neighboring buildings.

Temple Square was conceived to function as the center or hub of the city. Salt Lake City was literally laid out from the Temple Block as stipulated by Brigham Young. He saw the entire city as the theocratic center of the Church with the Temple as its spiritual center. Historic events prevented it from becoming a theocratically governed city. The Temple, however, does remain the spiritual center of The Church of Jesus Christ of Latter-day Saints as the envisioned "ensign to the nations from afar."

The Tabernacle is a masterpiece of engineering. Conceived by Brigham Young and built by Henry Grow, its elliptical dome rests on forty-four sandstone piers, spanning an area of 240 by 150 feet. It is the only permanent structure completed on Temple Square before Young's death in 1887. Henry Grow, a bridge builder, worked with a lattice arch truss system, constructing a span nine feet thick from ceiling to shingle. The timbers were ingeniously bound together. Where several crossed, holes were bored completely through and wooden dowels tightly driven in so as to extend on each side. The dowel ends were then split and wooden wedges driven in. The effect was the same as if the timbers had been tightly bolted together. The resonance of the chamber has remained superb. Wherever the timbers appeared weak they were tightly wrapped with wet rawhide strips. As the rawhide dried, the shrinking gave an effective reinforcement. Young also insisted that the plaster be thick; therefore, horsehair was used to give a strong knit to the plaster base, facilitating the application of heavy coats. With the addition of the free-standing gallery separated by two feet from the wall, the acoustical quality of the building was enhanced. Partway through the construction, Young decided to place the organ in the west end. The only organ builder available to Young providentially happened to be a master. Joseph Ridges spent twelve years on the task of creating an impressive instrument that has been expanded and changed over the years. The largest pipes today are 32-foot gold-leaf laminated pine, and sound at 16.35 cycles per second. The smallest pipes, less than ⅜ of an inch, sound at 16,744.03 cycles, with overtones to about 19,000. The first Tabernacle Choir was 150 voices, and the present Choir consists of 330. Church Architect William H. Folsom drew the first plans for the structure and Truman O. Angell, Sr., designed most of the interiors.

A view of the 375-seat choir area and the enlarged organ of 11,000 pipes at the west end of the Tabernacle.

The Seagull Monument by Mahonri Young commemorates the survival of the Saints in 1848 when seagulls devoured hordes of crickets that had descended on the crops.

Obed Taylor was appointed architect of the Assembly Hall soon after Brigham Young called for its construction on August 11, 1877. Henry Grow was appointed as the builder with Edward Brain, the master mason. Initially it was referred to as the "New Tabernacle," while the present building of that name was called the "Large Tabernacle." In December 1879, President John Taylor resolved the confusion that existed by officially calling it "The Salt Lake Assembly Hall." The sedate Victorian/Gothic building was completed in 1882 at a cost of $90,000. It is interesting to note that its original twenty-four finial spires were capped by exacting fiberglass shells while the center tower was rebuilt and repainted.

The Assembly Hall, since its dedication, has undergone a number of renovations. The exterior appearance has changed little except for the removal of a decorative balustrade and a four-foot-long weather vane reminiscent of the trumpeted angel once on the Nauvoo Temple. On the interior, the original ceiling murals that depicted temples and ancient and modern prophets were painted over while the three-tiered rostrum was altered. Between 1979 and 1983, the entire building underwent a complete and sympathetic restoration. Structural weaknesses associated with the roof trusses and center tower increased the difficulty and scope of the project. The result has been noteworthy. Besides the task of resolving the structural problems through the introduction of a concrete girth beam and a plywood diaphragm for the

ceiling, painstaking care has gone into the detail work. The painting, the stencil work, the regraining and the refinish of the softwood benches to give the appearance of oak and the wood columns the look of marble were done by skilled craftsmen. The focus of the interior is a new organ with 3,489 pipes. The acoustics were enhanced by attaching more than 800 speakers beneath the closely spaced benches in order that sound could bounce from the floor to the back of the front bench and then to the listener. The extensive restoration has preserved what some consider to be the architectural jewel of Temple Square.

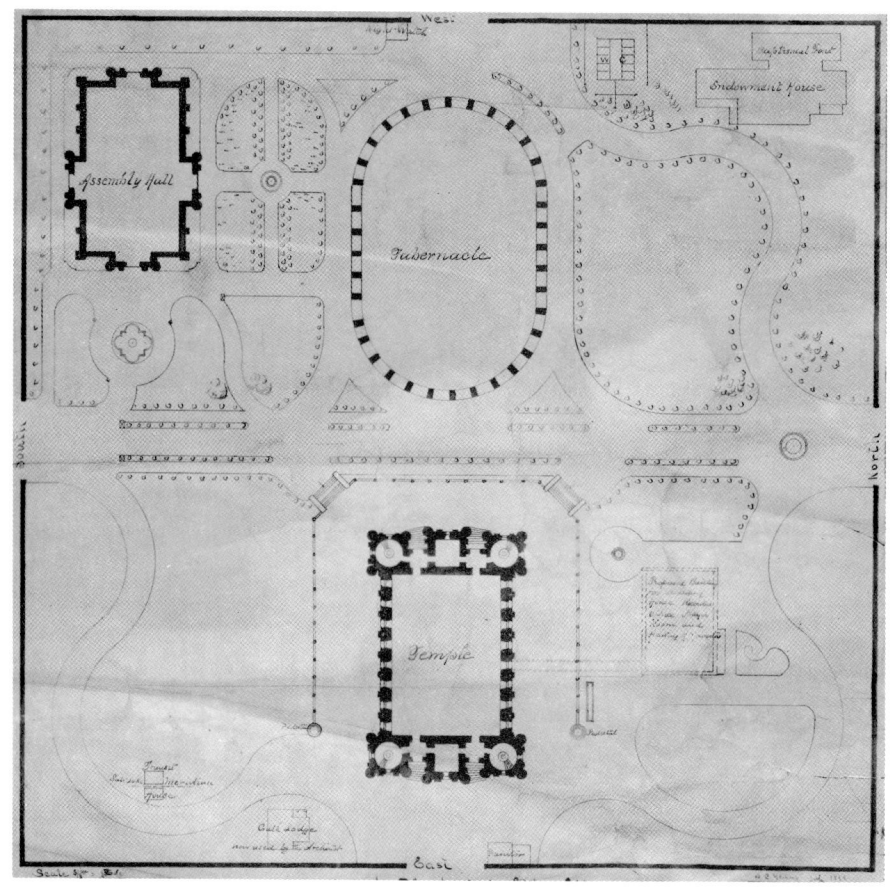

Above: The Temple Block (Square) as it appeared soon after the dedication of the Salt Lake Temple. The axial arrangement of the Temple and Tabernacle is evident with the Assembly Hall to the left and the Annex and Engine Room to the right. Upper right: The laying of the capstone on April 6, 1892, marked the completion of the exterior of the Temple. It was a day of jubilation for the Church. Soon after President Wilford Woodruff flipped the electric switch that lowered the capstone in place, the unified voices of some 40,000 people who had assembled on Temple Square to witness the event shouted, "Hosanna! Hosanna! Hosanna! to God and the Lamb! Amen! Amen! Amen!" which was repeated three times. The architect, Joseph Don Carlos Young, then declared that the capstone was laid, at which time the choir and congregation sang triumphantly the hymn The Spirit of God Like a Fire is Burning! Lower right: A view of the Salt Lake Temple as it appeared ca. 1890. Note Orson Pratt's adobe astronomical observatory on the southeast corner of the Temple Block, and the Tabernacle to the left of the Temple.

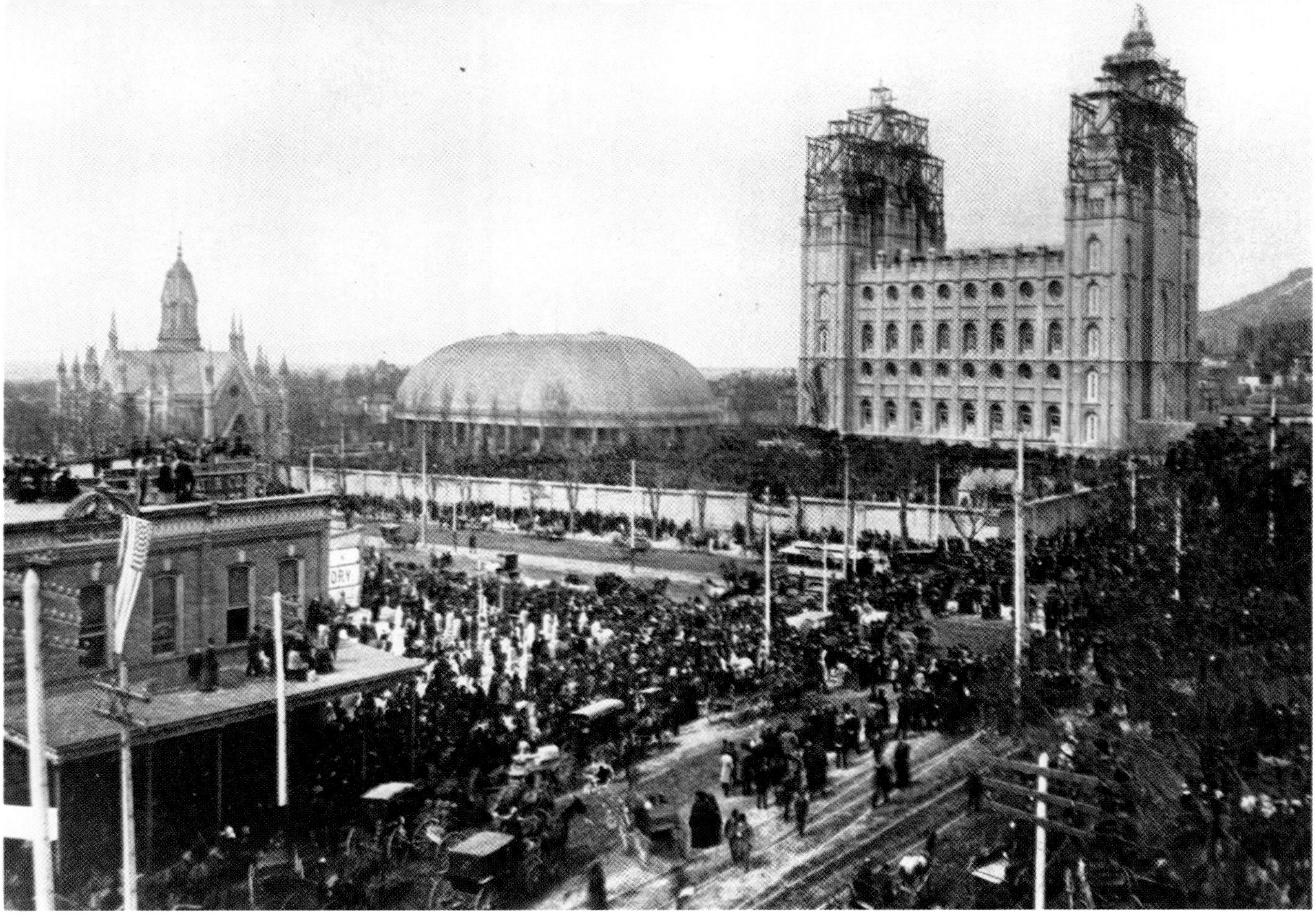

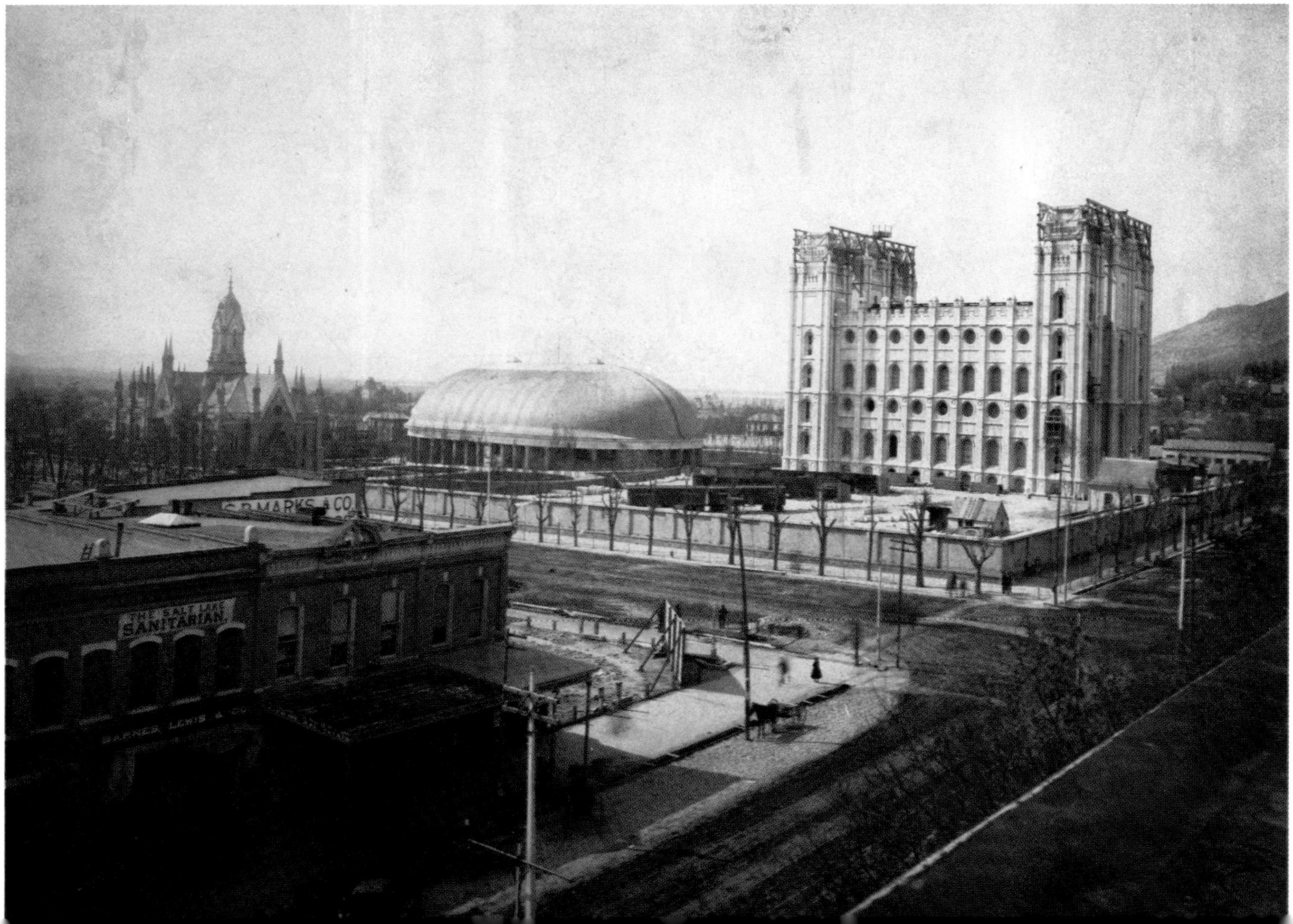

G.P. MARKS & CO.
THE SALT LAKE
SANITARIAN

Henry Grow, a bridge builder from Pennsylvania, was appointed by Brigham Young to supervise the construction of his proposed elliptical dome for the Tabernacle. His appointment was based on his knowledge and previous use of the Remington Patent for Lattice Bridges. (Brigham Young, no doubt, received inspiration for the dome from the "bent" truss used in the roof structure and the hemicycle apse of the Old Tabernacle. This is more plausible than the often cited "umbrella" and "egg shell" traditions.) The dome supplanted an earlier proposal for a quarter pitched roof with an attic as described by William H. Folsom, then acting Church Architect. Its original wooden shingles have been replaced twice—first with tin shingles and then by the present aluminum sheathing.

A view of the stone cutters and yard south of the Temple. The Endowment House is visible to the right of the Tabernacle.

Above and top right: A view of the Tabernacle interior as it appeared after the completion of the gallery and the organ, ca. 1871. The original organ bears a strong resemblance to one in the Boston Music Hall which Joseph Harris Ridges possibly saw while on a visit to that city in 1865-66 to purchase materials for his Tabernacle organ. The original organ contained 700 pipes, but through upgrading and renovation the number has increased to 11,000. Initially, five men worked the organ bellows, to be replaced by a water pump and eventually the present electrical system. Lower right: A view of the original 1852 adobe Tabernacle on the southwest corner of the Temple Block. To its right is the third Bowery to be erected on this site. It was constructed in 1854 to compensate for the limited seating capacity of the Tabernacle. The Bowery was razed in 1864 to make way for the present Tabernacle.

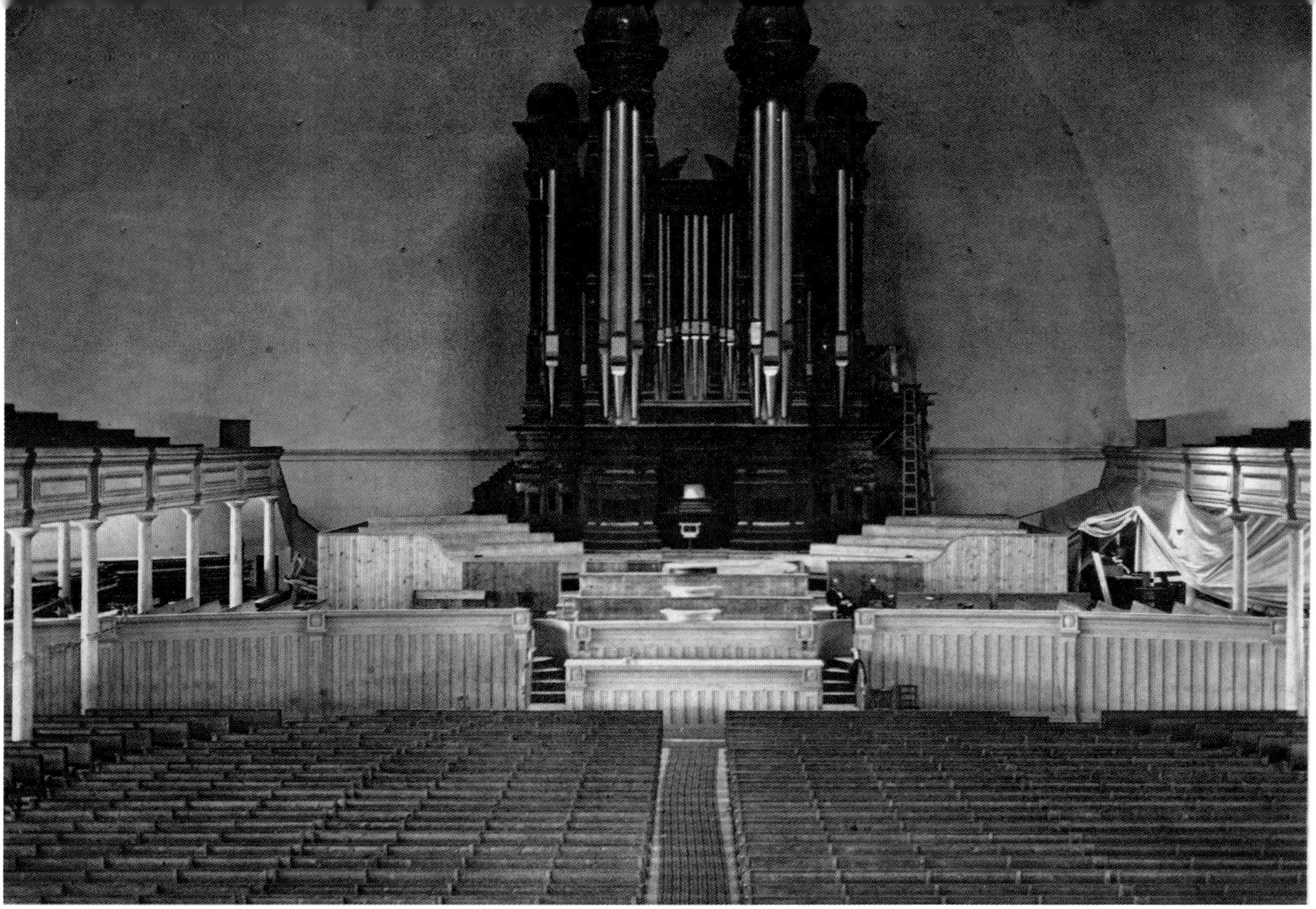

Upper right: Joseph Don Carlos Young's Byzantine-inspired Temple Annex (1892) was a stylistic departure from the architectural character of the Salt Lake Temple. It reflected his taste for the exotic and his knowledge of current trends in architecture. Lower right: Young's flair for the exotic was more evident in his design for the chimney stack of the Temple's heating plant (Engine Room).

Below: The Endowment House, built in 1854-1855 in the northwest area of the Temple Block, acted, in the words of Brigham Young, as a "temporary temple." For the next thirty-four years, the two-story adobe structure served in that capacity until it was razed in 1889 in preparation of the Salt Lake Temple assuming that responsibility.

ANNEX OF THE SALT LAKE TEMPLE.

A thin drawing of the original proposal for the Salt Lake Temple Annex. It was probably rendered by Truman O. Angell, Jr., before his release as the Temple architect. Its castellated style was more in sympathy with the design of the Salt Lake Temple than Joseph Don Carlos Young's completed annex.

VI
THE ARCHITECTURAL LEGACY

THE ARCHITECTURAL LEGACY

Even before its completion, the Salt Lake Temple had become the physical symbol of The Church of Jesus Christ of Latter-day Saints and of its triumph over adversity. The importance given the building by the Church membership is attributable to its prophetic origin and function. It is, as spoken by Isaiah, "the mountain of the Lord's house . . . in the tops of the mountains," from whence "shall go forth the law." With the passage of time, its function has eclipsed the significance of its architecture. Brigham Young envisioned it as a monument that would teach the faithful members of the Church and remind them of their responsibilities to themselves and to God.

The Salt Lake Temple is a compendium of LDS belief. Yet despite its monumental significance, it has had little influence on subsequent Church buildings, particularly the other nineteenth-century Utah temples. The St. George, Logan, and Manti Temples share a similar medieval character, but they differ in general configuration and lack symbolic content. Even the Washington, D.C. Temple, which was patterned directly from the Salt Lake Temple, exhibits little of its prototype's complexity and significance. The variance among these temples is appropriate because it preserves the symbolic importance and the individuality of the Salt Lake Temple—the most important building of The Church of Jesus Christ of Latter-day Saints.

The St. George Temple (1871-1877) was the only one of the four Utah temples proposed by Brigham Young to be completed before his death on August 29, 1877. Truman O. Angell, Sr., on President Young's request, designed a building patterned on the Nauvoo Temple. Since its dedication on April 6, 1877, it has undergone a number of renovations to the interior which have subsequently changed its original hall design except for the upper assembly hall. Fortunately, the exterior appears largely as completed, other than the tower which was enlarged following a fire set by a lightning bolt.

The Logan Temple (1877-1884) was designed by Truman O. Angell, Jr., under the direction of his father. It continued the castellated character of the Salt Lake Temple, but like the others, it does not exhibit overt exterior symbolism nor is it administratively important. The spatial movement of its interior served as the transition link between the hall pattern established by Joseph Smith and the circular pattern employed in the Salt Lake Temple. Unfortunately, this is no longer true due to a renovation and modernization program that completely changed the interior except for the upper assembly hall.

The Manti Temple (1877-1888) was designed by William H. Folsom under the direction of Truman O. Angell, Sr., which in part accounts for the similarity in design between it and the Logan Temple. Yet Folsom's architectural sensitivity and abilities were such that he produced what can be considered the most aesthetically refined of the early Utah temples. Fortunately, its original beauty and pioneer craftsmanship have been maintained through a program of thoughtful preservation.

The Washington, D.C. Temple (1971-1974) is a twentieth-century adaptation of the Salt Lake Temple. It was a collaborative design among the architects, Harold K. Beecher, Fred L. Markham, Keith W. Wilcox, and Emil B. Fetzer. Though monumental in size and wealth of materials, its machine image lacks a sense of sacrifice, devotion and venerability inherent in the original.

... We come before thee with joy and thanksgiving, with spirits jubilant and hearts filled with praise, that thou hast permitted us to see this day for which, during these forty years, we have hoped, and toiled, and prayed, when we can dedicate unto thee this house which we have built to thy most glorious name.... Today we dedicate the whole unto thee, with all that pertains unto it that it may be holy in thy sight; that it may be a house of prayer, a house of praise and of worship; that thy glory may rest upon it; that thy holy presence may be continually in it; that it may be the abode of thy Well-Beloved Son, our Savior; that the angels who stand before thy face may be the hallowed messengers who shall visit it, bearing to us thy wishes and thy will, that it may be sanctified and consecrated in all its parts holy unto thee, the God of Israel, the Almighty Ruler of mankind. And we pray thee that all people who may enter upon the threshold of this, thine house, may feel thy power and be constrained to acknowledge that thou hast sanctified it, that it is thy house, a place of thy holiness.... We bless thee, we praise thee, we glorify thee, we worship thee, day by day we magnify thee, and give thee thanks for thy great goodness towards us, thy children, and we pray thee, in the name of thy Son Jesus Christ, our Savior, to hear these our humble petitions, and answer us from heaven, thy holy dwelling place, where thou sittest enthroned in glory, might, majesty, and dominion, and with an infinitude of power which we, thy mortal creatures, cannot imagine, much less comprehend. Amen and Amen.*